Early Reviewers' P

MW01071582

The Reflections of Two 80-Year-Olds

THINKING THINGS OVER offers an opportunity to get to know two gifted people of very nearly the same age who grew up a few miles apart but first met each other when they were about 80 years old. Beautifully written with a charming sense of humor, this book is a pleasure to read.

W. John Glancy, retired attorney, former briefing clerk to U.S. Supreme Court Justice Byron White; Princeton, Yale Law School, and Oxford

This memoir is a story told through chatty narrative, emails, structured dialogue, and a play, all organized in a fascinating way. I had the feeling that I was sitting with two friends, looking through memorabilia as I listened to their life stories.

Elaine White, Ph.D., retired associate professor, The University of Southern Mississippi, and founding director of the Live Oak Writing Project

Charles Guittard and Nancy Davis Labastida's account of their long lives and their late-in-life marriage testifies to the resilience possible for all of us. Each recounts the trials and triumphs of more than eighty years lived separately. Nancy and Charles teach us all how to remain always young, never old.

Rabbi Mark L. Winer, MBE, Ph.D. (Yale), DD; American Interfaith Scholar and Activist; former senior rabbi, Western London Synagogue of British Jews; president of Foundation to Advance Interfaith Trust and Harmony

I was fascinated by your well-documented correspondence. I enjoyed what you've written, which has many parallels to my life. While the pace of your relationship was impressive, I did propose to Shirley a month after our first date.

Rev. Charles J. Castles, retired pastor, Presbyterian Church (USA); Rice University; life-long trumpet player and bandsman; previously with Procter & Gamble

---

Your memory for details is amazing. I do remember Miss Finley's, Bamboo Hall, bridge lessons, old-time radio shows, and the ophthalmologist in the Medical Arts Building downtown. I am certain writing this memoir was cathartic for both you and Nancy. BRAVO!

Cynthia (Cindy) Cousins Lodge, University of Nebraska and SMU, small business owner

---

I didn't like it. I loved it. There is only one word for it—delicious. Instead of reading it like a critic, I was totally taken up with it, wishing I had known you and Nancy better in high school. I feel we have so much in common, especially your comments about mothers and cultural development.

Madelyn (Maddy) Dolgoff Kamen, DrPH, Retired associate dean & professor, UT Health Science Center Houston; author of *Crazy Lady in the Mirror*

A rollicking good read and a view into the minds of a gifted writing team. And they have the distinct advantage of being in love with each other.

David E. Tripp, former district attorney & prosecutor L.A. County and USDOJ, vice president Spectra Vision, portrait & landscape painter

Such fun and such memories of a time that was softer and less complicated, a time when people enjoyed having fun without fearing for their lives. I loved Charles' notes on Dick Chaplin teaching us how to dance. Nancy's story about Ebb W. losing his contact in her strapless sequined dress as they danced was hilarious! Anyone who was around from 1955 to 1965 will adore the book.

Gloria Utay Solomon, award-winning former owner of event planning company and former officer of corporate management company

ALSO BY CHARLES FRANCIS GUITTARD

A Ph.D.'s Reverie

A Ph.D.'s Reverie: The Letters

I Will Teach History:
The Life & Times of Francis Gevrier Guittard,
Professor, Baylor University

Orthodontist Dr. Hurt tightens the wires in Charles' mouth.

Thinking Things Over
The Reflections of Two 80-Year-Olds

Charles Francis Guittard

Assisted by Nancy Davis Labastida
Illustrated by Amanda Hope Colborn
Edited by Georgette Taylor

THINKING THINGS OVER: The Reflections of Two 80-Year-Olds
Copyright ©2024 Charles Francis Guittard

ISBN 978-1506-911-67-0 CL
ISBN 978-1506-911-68-7 PBK
ISBN 978-1506-911-69-4 EBK
ISBN 978-1506-911-66-3 Supplement AUDIO

February 2024

Published and Distributed by
First Edition Design Publishing, Inc.
P.O. Box 17646, Sarasota, FL 34276-3217
www.firsteditiondesignpublishing.com

ALL RIGHTS RESERVED. No part of this book publication may be reproduced, stored in a retrieval system, or transmitted in any form or by any means — electronic, mechanical, photocopy, recording, or any other — except brief quotation in reviews, without the prior permission of the author or publisher.

A Note from the Author

Before the final sunset, can a self-conscious reclusive widower eighty years young find happiness and new life with an effusive widow and gregarious butterfly of eight decades? Can a man who can sneak up on you from the front hit it off with a woman you can hear talking coming around the corner? Can a guy sporting two left feet learn to dance with a gal of natural coordination and athleticism?

This short volume addresses those questions and others. It is composed of 4 pieces: an affectionate memoir entitled *How I Got Polished & What Happened After That*; a romantic piece entitled *"Wow, It's Almost Like We Walked Hand in Hand Through Our Childhood!" A Memoir of a Third Courtship & Marriage that Wasted No Time*; a piece entitled *"And Then There's the Time That..."* containing Nancy's best stories and memoir of growing up; and finally a bit of serious whimsy entitled *The Trial of J. Hiram Harmless: A Fantasy of a Final Judgment Day*.

The pieces were written mostly during the period I was casting about for a new writing project, and Nancy and I were both getting into the hang of a new marriage. The first gives proof that family and marriage matters remain central to my life; the second that neither of us wanted to live without romance; the third that Nancy is a born storyteller; and the fourth, that my legal background still occasionally creeps into my subconscious.

As to the first piece, one member of my family, who had not read my account of my parents' polishing efforts and was aware only of the title, had reservations about my going public on this subject. His concern was any suggestion that in my youth I was not always confident or possessing the desired social aplomb would be a mistake and I should avoid this subject. However, as I'm going for a little honesty and maybe some humor here, the memoir is unredacted. As Garrison Keillor said often on his radio show, "Powder-milk biscuits give shy persons the strength to get up and do what needs to be done." That aphorism has some application to the Guittard males, certainly to myself and at least the two generations preceding me. It may apply to those coming after. We owe it to those later Guittards to concede that we were not always as cool and awesome back then as we are today as fathers and grandfathers.

i

Those doubting the prospects for a late-life courtship of the sort described herein between your author and Nancy may be wondering:

- *Will* the widows on walkers and mah jongg players snag the widower at The Reserve, his residence in Dallas, Texas, before he is able to make his exit?

- *Will* the widow tire of his never-ceasing emails?

- *Will* there be a place for him, his books, and accumulated doodads, odds and ends, in her heart and house?

- *What* will their children and grandchildren think about their plan to marry?

- *Will* her many friends be able to accept their relationship? Or his car in her garage?

- *Will* he be able to relearn, after half a century, the game of contract bridge and the changes to the bidding rules?

Assisting in this effort is my third bride, confidant, and gentlest critic, the very perceptive Nancy Davis Labastida. Presented, for example, with my riddle for the day of why my unwashed T-shirt with toothpaste on the front yesterday showed no toothpaste spots today despite not having been put through the Maytag, she immediately answered correctly, "Because you put it on inside out." She solved instantly what I had been pondering standing in front of the mirror just moments before. May all the guys out there be blessed with wives who understand them that well!

Charles Francis Guittard
Austin, Texas

P.S. Final note: We have preferred to use pseudonyms or disguised names for some of the real people mentioned in this book. Those should be obvious from the text but can always be checked in the index at the conclusion of this work.

Thinking Things Over
The Reflections of Two 80-Year-Olds

CONTENTS

List of Illustrations

BY AMANDA HOPE COLBORN

How I Got Polished & What Happened After
That: Charles' Memoir of Growing Up

PART I

Mother's Areas—Manners, Music, Dancing, Bridge, and Others

My mother, Mary Lou Kee Guittard, was a polisher. So was Clarence, my father. They each had their special areas, although they collaborated in some of them, but initially it was mainly Mother. If she had an apple for a teacher, she would have spit-shined it before putting it on the teacher's desk. "First impressions are so important," she told us, and we heard it often. The raw materials on which she practiced her skills were her three children. The results of her polishing were not completely successful and certainly not always foreseeable, but that was not her fault. It was just the result of the materials she had to work with, and the fact that she was working in an area subject to many variables. The always mysterious inner workings of the individual human mind mean it is not always easy to foresee what effects will come from particular parental approaches, even when dealing with one's blood kin. This essay will address only my own case, not that of my siblings, and will indicate some of the ways my life has played out following Mother's earnest efforts to polish me. Some of the ways perhaps would have been predictable, others unpredictable. There have been high moments and low moments, with lessons learned during the polishing. All her polishings have contributed to who I am and where I am today. One thing I have learned for sure, whatever the attempts of your parents for your improvement, you can never be absolutely sure what will come in the wake of those efforts.

A few words about Mother herself. She was well polished by her mother, Mary Louise Roscoe Kee ("Louise" herein), a refined woman from Kentucky who became prominent in Waco ladies' clubs after her marriage to John Lester Kee, MD. Louise, a bit of a

3

poet, was a fan of Kahlil Gibran's *The Prophet*, which was popular for decades beginning in 1923. Mother herself was president of several clubs where she presided and introduced the speaker of the day. Because Mother was not a natural speaker and neither effusive nor especially talkative, public speaking was an exercise she did after diligent practice. On one occasion, I could hear her at the dining room table going over her planned words of introduction for a speaker— "It is a *special* pleasure that...," "It is a *very* special pleasure that...," "It is *so* special that...," and other slightly different but substantially similar ways ad infinitum of saying exactly the same thing. Mother was after perfection, but knowing absolutely the best way to say something was always elusive. One eerie moment shedding light on Mother's ongoing attempt to polish me occurred on a family trip to see her Kee cousins in Mississippi. These cousins of Mother's were poor country people without many of the benefits Mother was accustomed to, having been brought up by educated parents and a father with a successful medical practice. One cousin was a young woman almost a dead ringer for Mother. The most obvious difference was her noticeably snaggle-toothed mouth, which surely would have given pause to any neighborhood swains needing a date to the school hayride. Mother would have been saddened at the condition of her poor relative's teeth.

Mother was not only accomplished in her manners and everyday etiquette, but also in the niceties of parliamentary procedure which involves motions, votes, points of order and clarification, and a great deal of politeness. One of the ladies' clubs Mother was trying to keep alive, despite its declining popularity, was devoted to the study of parliamentary procedure. In a sense, Mother's support of the study was also a mission of kindness to an older friend who had a passion for teaching this subject. The club often met at our house, with Mother having set out on the dining room table coffee, tea, and little cookies or cakes. After fortifying themselves against a strong dose of parliamentary procedure to be administered by Mrs. Harding, the ladies—a very small group—repaired to the living room where chairs had been set up to accommodate what was gradually becoming a thinner and thinner crowd. One time, as I listened at the top of the stairs, I could tell that Mrs. Harding was not pleased with her devoted little group. They had not done their homework studying their handouts. I was just in time to hear Mrs. Harding wail pitifully, "Ladies, I work so hard to prepare for my lectures for you. Why won't you read your materials for our meetings? I don't know why I even try...." After that, you could have heard a pin drop.

Where my father was concerned, my mother's code of manners extended to the husband-wife relationship to an unrealistic degree. Having been brought up in an age or perhaps household in which feelings were not usually openly expressed, especially negative feelings, Mother was truly a product of her times. On one occasion, I heard the end of an unusual conversation. My parents were having a disagreement in the hearing of her children about something, the nature of which was not clear to me, the only disagreement of theirs I ever heard out in the open. The argument had already been going on for a while when I heard Mother say, "C [her pet name for my father, Clarence], Use your *sweet* voice." Father weakly responded, "Does my voice always have to be sweet?" To that, Mother responded emphatically, "Always." That ended their little dust up, at least the part I could hear. This story never fails to bring a smile to the faces of my brother and sister.

Mother's wardrobe was extensive and carefully selected for quality and price. She didn't pick up bargains at the Goodwill store, or, insofar as I know, at the Neiman Marcus remnant sales, although she loved Neiman Marcus and its Zodiac Room restaurant. After the kids moved out, her clothes filled four closets with coordinated ensembles hanging neatly in plastic sacks side by side, smelling of mothballs. Her jewelry was tasteful, although not pricey—Father was an insurance defense and railroad lawyer and later a judge, not a big bucks personal injury plaintiffs' attorney. As an attorney, he made a dependable but not unusually high salary as an attorney defending the bus company, the railroad, and other companies in relatively low-dollar lawsuits. He also brought eminent domain actions all over Texas when a client needed right-of-way across private property. He was not a plaintiffs' attorney earning contingent fees in large injury cases. Despite the fact that she was never dripping in diamonds or designer suits, Mother always looked immaculate when she presided at club meetings. She had hair salon appointments every week for many years to have her hair styled in a new permanent. I've always wondered why the word "permanent" was used. A better name would have been "now you see it, tomorrow you won't hair treatments."

Children after birth, it's true, not only require food, shelter, clothing, and inoculation against scary diseases including smallpox, diphtheria, whooping cough, tetanus, and polio, but many other attentions. Romulus and Remus may have been raised with a pack of wolves, but Mary Lou Guittard's children would not be. I will relate the various areas in which Mother attempted to polish me and perhaps my siblings and some of the ways Father did, as well. Polishing is not an exact science they both would have admitted, the results always being somewhat uncertain. At some point, the polishee is on his own, floundering around and fending for himself in situations where he or she must figure things out the hard way, or, in some cases, completely on the fly.

The areas in which Mother focused her attention were manners, piano and art lessons, ballroom dancing, bridge, public speaking, appearance, health, and, indirectly, socializing with young women. Father's areas were Boy Scouts (a weak area), reading and writing (his strongest emphases), and tennis and golf (he tried but was not athletically gifted). Finally, sex (a tricky subject he was uncomfortable with), and moral and spiritual guidance (another of his long suits).

The first area that Mother began her polishing was in manners, particularly table manners. Not talking while chewing was high on her list, keeping one's mouth closed while chewing, saying "Please pass the [whatever]," "May I be excused?", keeping my elbows off the table ("Mabel, Mabel, strong and able, keep your elbows off the table!"), always spearing a piece of meat with the fork in my right hand after transferring the fork from my left after cutting off a piece of meat using a knife and fork, and other admonitions on table behavior. These lessons were supported by several long play 78 records Mother had from the brain of Frank Luther, an apparent favorite of hers called *Manners Can be Fun*. Mr. Luther's little melodies were catchy, and although I never thought of using them with my own kids, I can still sing some of his little songs— "Oh, we say please and thank you. It's such a pleasant thing to do..."

My manners training under Mother certainly didn't hurt after I was drafted into the U.S. Army after law school. Saying "Yes, Sir" was advisable in the Army when addressing superiors—and that meant nearly everybody—instead of "Okay" or "Let me think about that, Sergeant." I should have remembered Frank Luther's little song on saying please and thank you, which would have spared me a little embarrassment as I was being discharged for medical reasons after thirty-seven days at Fort Polk, Louisiana. The problem was that on the day of my discharge, I put on my olive Jack Nicklaus golf jacket on top of my green uniform—the colors were very similar was my thinking—and was publicly chastised by some non-commissioned officer to remove my jacket immediately, which I did politely and without audible complaint. I had failed to ask anyone in authority, "Please sir, would it be acceptable if I wear my Jack Nicklaus jacket since I'm going home today?" That would have gone nowhere fast I'm sure, but who knows? It was worth a try and Mother would have been proud.

My piano lessons and time sitting on a wooden piano bench without a cushion were mercifully brief. My first teacher was Mrs. Stanley when I was in elementary school. I don't think Mrs. Stanley liked children that much, as her method of teaching them how to play staccato, for example, was less than subtle. As I was practicing on a keyboard that made no sound—yes, a soundless keyboard! — she came along and whacked my hands up from underneath to make sure I was quickly raising my hands after hitting an imaginary note on a soundless keyboard. If you've ever played the game of "slappy handy" with your friends, you understand what we were all experiencing. And that soundless keyboard! It seemed to me then and seems to me now an unmusical way to teach piano technique. Music, I always thought, is about making musical sounds.

After I served out my sentence with Mrs. Stanley, Mother signed me up for regular lessons with Erna Renard Radke, a well-known private teacher living in our neighborhood. Mrs. Radke was a kind and encouraging teacher, there was no soundless keyboard, and she did not slap my hands. That was a good start. I stayed a couple of years with Mrs. Radke and performed at a couple of recitals, one in which I played a duet, "A Salute to the Colors," with my younger brother, John. John would later go on to far eclipse my efforts on the piano as Mother found him post-Mrs. Radke a fine teacher of adults to ensure he didn't drop out too soon after Mrs. Radke. I dropped out because I didn't like the drudgery of playing scales and other pieces endlessly in daily practice that always lasted at least thirty minutes when I always wanted to be doing something else. My earliest achievement at the piano was playing "From a Wigwam"—you can find it on YouTube—and my last achievement was a piece I played at recital time, "Rustic Dance." Since my last recital in 1953, I have played "Rustic Dance" by muscle memory countless times through the years until gradually I was remembering less and less and then much later only the right hand without the left-hand accompaniment. I can still play a little, but I run out of notes in less than a minute. One little admission—I have played "slappy handy" with my kids, but only as a game and not to teach them how to play an instrument. It never made their hands red—not too red anyway.

By the way, neither Mother nor Father ever sat down at the piano with me and played anything themselves; they could have if either had remembered how to play, although Father probably could have produced a reasonable sound from a French horn. They had generously invested in a serviceable piano for us, not a baby grand, but certainly adequate for beginners. I guess they just thought it would help to polish me if I could do something they had never really learned themselves. I did benefit from my years with the piano. By the time I was old enough to play a band instrument, I could read music and knew all about sharps and flats, time signatures, quarter notes and eighth notes, and other essential things. As to the piano, I never developed my piano talent sufficiently to play either "Heart and Soul" or "Country Gardens" with a partner in a duet. Those old standards, also on YouTube, would have been great to know and play. They were very popular at the time, although at some point they were played too often, and nearby adults were probably cringing. But as I said, I did learn how to dance and to play in the school band, and I also learned to play tennis and bridge, all of which I will come to directly.

Mother did decide early on that I had at least some artistic talent and thought I should develop it. After all, in elementary school and high school I was often drawing on whatever paper was handy (or the programs at church), and I would bring home refrigerator-worthy pictures. I was one of the three best artists in my elementary class of thirty kids, although I thought two of my classmates' pictures were actually better than mine. Corky McCord could draw great battle scenes with soldiers and football scrimmages with cool-looking players, and Tommy Blackshear could draw funny pictures of Indians. Despite their apparent superiority as cartoonists, I was somehow selected as the artist for my sixth-grade class. Our class put out a mimeographed Christmas newsletter that featured a drawing of Santa, his sleigh, and his reindeer on the front page. However, after the issue was mimeographed and passed around, it was obvious that the teacher had not cared for my depiction of Santa's head and had inserted another head. I did not like the new head. Despite this early setback and rebuke, I continued to draw for many years. In my tenth-grade speech class, I drew ten caricatures of unsuspecting students which were actually pretty good. Mother's contribution to all this mild outbreak of talent was to sign me up for art lessons at the downtown YMCA. There, I produced a few serious pencil sketches that weren't half bad.

My introduction to dancing occurred in Mrs. Finley's dance studio when I was in the eighth grade. I don't remember much about those sessions except that I am reminded of Penrod Schofield's experience with dance lessons described in *Penrod,* a book Father encouraged me to read years before I actually read it. Although I don't remember much about Mrs. Finley's dance lessons, I do remember the lessons from Dick Chaplin, a longtime Dallas dance entrepreneur and Arthur Murray graduate, who organized dance classes for secondary school students. Chaplin included not just the basic ballroom dances but also the bunny hop and other popular dances of the times, including the bop. The dirty bop, a mildly suggestive dance by today's standards, was not taught or allowed. Lessons in the dirty bop would have been problematic for me in any event as I've never felt comfortable moving in an uninhibited sexy way—Elvis the Pelvis I was not. I liked the lessons with Chaplin though, and I still remember the attractive assistant who helped him demonstrate the various dances.

It is a fact, however, that one unfortunate thing occurred as a result of my being in that class. A tall but very nice girl in my class named Millie, who had been one of my dance partners, invited me to be her date at a birthday party for her at a country club. I told her I would like to, but that I had a Latin Club banquet the same night and the timing might be a problem. She said it was okay to just go to the party when the banquet was over, and we made the date. As it turned out, the banquet commenced at 5:30 and around 8:00, as I was preparing to leave the banquet for Millie's party, one of the teachers—probably my teacher, Mrs. Hamilton—was about to announce the awards for Latin proficiency. Seeing I was getting up to leave, another teacher told me I needed to stay for the awards but didn't say why. I stayed, and the Latin awards were announced slowly and one at a time. By the time it was announced that I had won one of the top awards, a little pre-printed yellow ribbon, it was too late to drive out to Millie's party. I called Millie's house and talked to her mother, explaining what had happened, but I never talked to Millie. I never saw her again, as the lessons at Dick Chaplin's had concluded. I've always felt I ruined her big night. Maybe she had someone else to dance with at her party, but I will never know. Hopefully, she was not traumatized for life and didn't have to talk to a therapist about it years later. Thinking about it today, I don't know why I didn't buy her a little gift and take it over to her.

Band and then orchestra filled in the gap when I gave up on piano lessons. Band was Father's main extracurricular activity at Waco High and at Baylor, and debate after band. He played French horn and is shown in his band uniform in old family photos. I did not play a band instrument at the time, but a neighborhood friend of mine—Dick Sartain, son of an SMU business school professor—was already playing sousaphone in the Highland Park Junior High beginning band. A sousaphone was a relatively easy band instrument to play, and if I could learn the sousaphone, getting in the band would be a snap. The heavy, cumbersome horn was not a sexy instrument like the trumpet or the snare drum where I would have had a lot of competition for a band spot at Highland Park Junior High. A very good band, by the way. I was right about that but not focused in on another thing: those special chairs in the band room that supported a metal (not fiberglass) sousaphone—which weighed around fifty-five pounds—were of no help when marching as it had to be carried over the shoulder by young bandsmen. The good news is I could stay after school to learn my scales and qualify for the top band for the following semester. I was very excited about that as the top band wore fairly new uniforms (red and orange) which looked very sharp to this seventh grader. I would be wearing one the next year, or so I thought.

The bad news is that by staying after school to practice scales on the sousaphone, I had to catch the bus home (no big deal by itself). However, I had the bad luck to fall prey to a couple of ne'er-do-well ninth graders who thought it would be a good use of their time to intimidate and punch me as I waited for the bus. It started when I was standing at the bus stop on Hillcrest; I heard a voice calling out "Don't look at us." As I could see no one, I curiously started looking around, finally noticing a couple of students up in a tree. As I pondered why they were up in the tree and why they did not want to be seen, they scrambled down the tree and came directly over to me. At that point, they reminded me of their command not to look at them, and the shorter guy, who seemed to be the leader, grabbed me. I resisted effectively, as I was a husky youth used to wrestling during playground time at elementary school. However, the taller guy, seeing that his companion needed assistance, then grabbed me from behind while the shorter guy started punching me in the stomach, whaling on me until he got tired.

That experience substantially spoiled the rest of my seventh-grade days at Highland Park Junior High. I had to be careful about finding rides home, which was not always possible. I also did have a lucky shirt—lucky only because on the days I wore this shirt, I hadn't run into either of those guys in the school hallways or outside the school. I learned later that a similar but much worse thing had happened to Mike W–, a seventh grade and Boy Scout friend of mine who got in a schoolyard fight with a ninth grader. Later that week, I saw Mike walking around the school with several large red and blue goose eggs on his head, which was a pretty weird and scary look. After getting beat up, Mike bravely and gamely decided on revenge and immediately began a program of bodybuilding and perhaps fight training. After a period of hard work, he challenged the ninth grader to a re-fight and, according to all reports, really worked the guy over with fists powered by his pumped-up muscles. Mike was now quite a muscular guy.

In my case, it would take six years and I would be in law school learning to be a courtroom fighter before I embarked on learning karate. At a studio near the law school, I had four lessons from high-level black belt entrepreneur Allen Steen and mentally rehearsed how I could take out people within reach of my chops should that become necessary. It also seemed obvious that on any given day, without regard to the bus stop bullies, I could be within punching distance of another knucklehead bully. By the time, however, I had finished the short course in karate, the taller of the two guys who had spoiled the rest of my seventh grade was found swinging from a rafter in the attic of his parents' home. I had mixed emotions when I heard that, but I admit my first emotion was deeply felt "Yes, there is a God" satisfaction. The second was wondering if he had been bullied by his father or older brother, and that, along with whatever else was bothering him, resulted in his self-destructive demise. I never saw the shorter guy again, although I doubt I would have aggressively challenged him like Mike did his antagonist. Mike had taken some serious lumps and I had not. I have never had an occasion to use the karate chops I learned in 1965, and at this late date, I am just banking on not waiting at bus stops on street corners where there are hooligans hiding up in nearby trees.

Mother facilitated my interest in bridge, a card game and handy social skill, when I was in high school, probably as a junior. She and Father both played a little bridge. Truth be told, they were both near beginners, had never had serious lessons for any length of time, and played infrequently with other weak players. Mother had taken a course from Mrs. Herbert Wales, and when she played, she kept a blue folder of instructions open on her lap so she could flip through it. That tended to slow her bidding and her play of the hand down to a crawl. They had both played the popular game of canasta with friends; my brother and I first played canasta with them before we played bridge. Before bridge, I was already playing gin rummy, hearts, spades, poker, casino, and blackjack with a group of high school guys, which included an assortment of debaters, bandsmen, math brains, and miscellaneous add-ons. We always had maybe a dollar riding on the results of our games to make them more interesting. We also played in our homes where we could be assured of card tables, cold drinks, snacks, and bathroom access. There were no girls, and there were no little brothers or sisters running around. It seems unlikely, but maybe girls didn't play bridge in high school back then—I never heard of any. Some of the guys in our all-guy group were already playing bridge, and there was an interest already there when I started playing with the guys.

Not all my card friends took bridge lessons, but the ones who did immediately had a leg up. The math brains who felt they didn't need to spring for the modest cost of lessons soon fell back in the standings as they played by the seat of their pants without guidance from any organized system like Goren (dominant system at the time), Culbertson, or Sheinwold. It seems that naked math brains were no match for ordinary brains who had inhaled Goren. Charles Goren was king of bridge teachers and writers; at home we had a copy of Goren's 1950s book (around 300 pages) which I read from cover to cover. The lessons were conducted at our house by a pleasant little woman Mother found named Nancy Touchstone, who provided written handouts for each lesson. During the summer of 1960, after my senior year in high school, we played bridge all summer long in air-conditioned homes, abandoning all other card games and also our miniature golf outings to local courses. Although I was no math genius, I was arguably the most serious student of bridge—if that can be measured by the amount of reading I did to learn the game and sharpen my bidding and hand-playing skills. That reading included the bridge column in the paper by a member of the Dallas Aces (Bobby Wolff), perhaps the U.S.'s foremost duplicate team at that time. Later, I would learn that Henry Baer of McKenzie & Baer, the first law firm that offered me a job, was a fine player and did legal work for Ira Corn, one of the Aces and a top guy at Michigan General. Sidebar comment: I would also learn that Bill McKenzie, my other boss at McKenzie & Baer, who was not known to be a bridge player, reportedly served under General George Patton. According to McKenzie's obituary, Bill was the first American soldier to enter Buchenwald Concentration Camp at the end of WWII.

The bridge games we played at each other's houses were fun in high school, but one session was marked by a distressing incident. One session at Jerry G's house, Dexter B– required a nature call, Dexter stumbling in on Jerry's mother planted firmly on the toilet. News of this happening produced loud laughter at our two bridge tables, perhaps from everyone except Jerry, who must have identified with his had-to-have-been mortified mother. We continued to play, and our hostess (Jerry's mother) made no appearance before the end of our session. Some wag on the spot felt compelled to quote Alexander Pope's line all of us had learned in senior English: "Fools rush in where angels fear to tread," naturally evoking more raucous laughter at Dexter's expense. There is something about guys and bathroom humor.

I don't know if the cringy episode at Jerry's house in some strange way may have had something to do with a later and more serious breach of bridge norms. On the day in question, Dexter and Burt A– were partners at Dexter's house, and I was playing with someone whose name is lost to history. As usual, we each had our glasses of iced Coca-Cola and Dr. Pepper on the card table—a rather light and insubstantial fold-up type it would turn out—along with bowls of a tasty garlic mayonnaise dip, a specialty of Dexter's mother. I don't remember the bidding, but Dexter opened in some suit, and Burt took him to a foolish game contract in Dexter's suit, which should have been doubled by me or my partner and perhaps was. The player on Dexter's left then made the opening lead, and Burt laid down the dummy, the hand upon which he had taken Dexter to game. Instantly, the usual calm and spirit of bonhomie which had been maintained up until then was shattered by a series of events not seen before or since in the Western world. Dexter, looking at the pitiful dummy hand Burt put down, realized in a flash that Burt did not have the points to take Dexter to game and was inexcusably short of trumps and other points. The situation was that Dexter did not only have the slightest chance of making the contract bid by Burt, but he would be going down by several tricks and piling up a lot of points for our side. In a fit of white-hot anger and frustration, seeing inevitable humiliation if he played out the hand, Dexter took immediate action: Spitting oaths at Burt, Dexter came down with both fists on the table—cards, drinks, chips, and dip flew everywhere, and a big pool of dark soda pop quickly accumulated on the table. Dexter then started picking up the wet cards, tearing them in two, and throwing them up in the air, the pungent aroma of garlic everywhere.

As one might imagine, this incident could not be laughed off with the players simply resuming bridge with a new deck of cards and a dried-off card table. One would have supposed that Dexter would have then simply exited the room to sulk while the rest of us could hastily dodge out the front door. But before any of that could happen, Dexter, with sulking the farthest thing from his mind, challenged Burt to go outside and box in Dexter's garage with gloves supplied by Dexter. Burt, leery of Dexter's threat and knowing that Dexter was beyond mildly upset yet afraid to back down after being challenged in front of peers, reluctantly accompanied Dexter to the garage. Once in the garage and after donning boxing gloves, Burt presumably took the kind of unequal pounding that can occur when one party is out of control (Dexter) and the other party (Burt) timidly defends himself against a raging antagonist. Suffice it to say, there is no record that Dexter and Burt ever played bridge as partners again. Perhaps this sad story is a predictable consequence of Burt's mother not polishing him with bridge lessons or Dexter's mother not teaching him not to tear up bridge cards when upset at a partner's bid. Dexter's mother should have also advised Dexter that bridge is for fun, not a blood sport, and not to work out personal grievances when a hand goes bad.

One more story about Dexter and Burt at a time when they were actually friends probably happened before the fight in the garage. One of them had a science project in biology which required an animal's skeleton. I don't know the details of this project, did not take biology, and can only assume. One of them said something along the lines of "Let's do a rabbit—I have a little rabbit my parents gave me for Easter." That much information by itself would have given almost anyone pause and then send him looking for the SPCA's phone number. However, Dexter and Burt paused not and settled on the unmown vacant lot at the end of our block to dispatch the hapless Easter rabbit. They planned to take the rabbit and an implement of some kind, a shovel or a hammer, to kill the rabbit if all else failed. I have no idea what other possibly more humane or animal-friendly lethal measures may have been debated for dispatching the rabbit. In the vacant lot, it finally came down to hitting the rabbit repeatedly with a heavy metal implement. In other words, blunt force trauma. As I recall hearing the story later from one of them, probably Burt, Dexter took the lead in terminating the life of the sacrificial Easter bunny, with repeated blows to the little rabbit, and there were many as the rabbit just would not stop squealing. Unfortunately, there was so much damage done to the rabbit's skeleton it was no longer suitable for a science project. As sad and grotesque as this episode was, I have a hard time not smiling a little, as it is wired in my brain along with Elmer Fudd singing, "Kill the wabbit, kill the wabbit," the "wabbit" in question being Bugs Bunny, one of my favorite cartoon characters.

My bridge lessons and summer sessions with my buddies prepared me well for serious bridge later at Baylor and in Waco, Texas, where I played duplicate with my roommate Larry A– at the way-past-its-prime Raleigh Hotel. Larry cautiously played under an alias as his strict Baptist parents would not have been pleased with his improving his bridge game at a seedy old hotel playing against townies instead of spending every spare moment conjugating Latin verbs or reading his Sunday School quarterly. His relationship with his parents seemed at the time to be a little strained as he accepted, but did not eat, the loaves of homemade banana bread his mother gave him each time he left home to return to Baylor. Ten to twenty loaves, all wrapped lovingly in tinfoil, were neatly stacked on a shelf on his side of the closet like bricks in a chimney. I always liked banana bread—still do—but although I could have eaten my fill from any loaf in that stack, I never wanted to try any of those unrefrigerated loaves. Keeping them stacked up like that and never taking a bite, Larry seemed to be venting feelings of resentment toward his parents for I don't know what. Maybe he was just trying to escape a closely monitored Southern Baptist upbringing by his pastor father and his mother and was secretly mocking his heritage. Maybe he was trying to lose weight. Possibly he didn't like banana bread. Nope, everyone likes banana bread.

But back to bridge—whether in Waco, Dallas, or elsewhere, I played in a few games where some players did not remember that bridge is for fun. Wives would harangue husbands for bad bidding or bad play of hands, and fathers would mock sons for boneheaded bids and plays. Maybe a dose of Mrs. Touchstone would have helped, known for saying never "whynch" your partner.

PART II

More of Mother's Areas—Speech, Scouts, and Conversation; and Father's Areas—Debate, Tennis and Golf, Reading and Writing, Geography, and Others

Three areas for my improvement are related: speech training, competitive debating, and becoming comfortable talking to the fair sex. Mother, having a major interest in all of these areas, knew that since I was the oldest of her three children, any steps or missteps of mine in these areas could be important for any who might follow me. First, Mother lined up a private speech teacher named Mrs. Bushman, although not a speech therapist, as I did not lisp or have a lazy tongue or a problem reading or saying words. Rather, for me it was always a matter of confidence when it came to speaking. Mrs. Bushman's program included performing memorized pieces and building vocabulary. For vocabulary, I kept a stenographic notebook and listed the new words I had found in books, magazines, or newspapers. I received Mrs. Bushman's award for the student who learned the most new words and could pronounce them correctly. There were one or two speech recitals at her house in which students recited pieces from memory while their anxious mothers kept their fingers crossed—rather like the recitals of Mrs. Radke's piano students at Mrs. Radke's house mentioned earlier. I followed up on this training by signing up in the tenth grade at Hillcrest for a speech course taught by Paul Evangeline Pettigrew. Among other speech assignments, I wrote a little play in which I read all the parts; Mr. Pettigrew, or PEP as we sometimes called him, thought it was mildly humorous, the title being *Boy & Girl Relationships in Foreign Lands*. I created it out of thin air since I had no relationships with girls in foreign lands other than a pen pal in the sixth grade which hardly deserves mention. We wrote a few letters back and forth and that was it. In another piece, I interviewed other class members in front of the class. Mr. Pettigrew liked my no-nonsense interviewer style. I did feel this speech class represented an important early breakthrough in my confidence building, but I still had a long way to go.

In the eleventh grade, I signed up for debate under Mr. Pettigrew and got in a lot of practice that year debating with different partners in tournaments before judges who were adults I did not know. I was always anxious when I got up to make my speeches. Anxiety sometimes translated to trips to the restroom. At a practice round with students from Ursuline Academy (a Catholic girls' prep school) before the round began, I visited the boys' restroom. Absentmindedly, I did not notice as I closed the stall door that the toilet paper dispenser was empty. Fortunately, however, there were no other students there that afternoon and I was able to hop from one stall to the next. That was a learning experience. I had a learning experience of the confidence-building sort during my junior year on a long ride back from a tournament. Our teams grabbed a bite to eat at a roadside greasy spoon and I happened to say something in a dry manner—I have no idea what—as we waited for our burgers to be brought out from the greasy spoon's kitchen. One of the older, better debaters thought my remark was funny. I had not realized I could occasionally be funny extempore, even if it was by accident.

At some point during my senior year, I finally connected with a regular debate partner—Jerry G–, also a senior, a clarinet player in the band with me, and one of my regular bridge buddies (whose mother I mentioned earlier)—and we had some success. Actually, on one occasion earlier in the year when I was paired with a sophomore named Eddie for a practice debate, we took on another Hillcrest team which included a member of the Hillcrest team that won the state championship in boys' debate later that year. As I recall, Eddie and I came out well in that practice debate, as I had craftily done some research in back issues of *U.S. News & World Report* and developed an unusual argument for the affirmative side about the need to ban the union-enforced practice of feather-bedding. The argument caught our opponents flat-footed, and they had no response. None. I always felt masterful when the other side couldn't think of anything to say to rebut a surprise argument of mine.

Tournament competition was always a challenge for my GI tract. At one tournament, my partner—an up-and-coming sophomore debater named Robert whose briefcase I inherited after he dropped debate—and I were miraculously undefeated after five straight rounds. While we were nervously waiting for results outside the auditorium where the scores were being tabulated, the tension was so great I became nauseated and was compelled to quickly find a trash can and hurl. And hurl I did, notwithstanding any amused gawkers standing around. One source of my anxiety could have been my hastily packed wardrobe that weekend. In my rush for the road trip to Midland, Texas, I had brought a shirt with French cuffs but alas no cufflinks. I also forgotten to take my black dress shoes and just brought along my white buck band shoes. I can't recall how any of that could have happened. Once in Midland, though, I realized the wardrobe predicament I was in and, as a last-minute substitute for cufflinks, found somewhere some string and jerry-rigged the cuffs of each sleeve together. Now the problem was, not having scissors, the white strings were visible dangling out of my cuffs which hung from my coat sleeves. However, there was nothing I could do about not having black shoes. Removing my white bucks— great for marching on the football field but not for a debate tournament—and debating in my socks would been distracting to the judges, notwithstanding my sharp dark suit and flashy gold vest. Debating in my socks would have drawn attention to my feet instead of my arguments. However, debating in white bucks with strings dangling was not fatal, and we had won every round before I committed my troubles to that trash can.

The high point of my high school debating career was at a big tournament my senior year in Brownwood, Texas, at Howard Payne University. Jerry G– and I did well in the final round for the championship against a smooth, well-dressed team from Houston Kinkaid High School, both Kinkaid students going on to careers as outstanding attorneys. For that tournament, Jerry and I had agreed that I would make the first and last of the affirmative's four speeches and Jerry the second and third speeches. I liked making the last affirmative speech (the rebuttal) since the team on the negative side would not be allowed to respond under standard debate rules. We took the championship and a nice trophy by a 4-1 decision; the trophy was later relocated from a display case at school to my room at home, and then consigned to the attic after I left home. I have always wondered if we lost that one vote because my still-changing voice cracked in my final speech, going from my baritone to a falsetto and back down again as I fast-talked for five minutes demolishing (I would like the think) the other team's arguments.

As an eighty-year-old thinking back, I realize that although I improved in my speaking and confidence from all my speech and debate training, I never became completely fluent or confident. My father, many of whose speaking genes I must have inherited and who had some speaking and debate training, also never became a smooth speaker. His métier was the written word, which recorded his clear and logical legal reasoning and fitted him perfectly for his eventual role as an appellate justice who crafted six hundred polished and reasoned opinions. As a speaker, though, he was never polished and was always a bit herky-jerky, as if revising his choice of words, phrases, and sentences on the fly as he went along. His speaking style always made me a little nervous when I listened to him give a speech at the bar association or to a Sunday school class. His legal analysis was exceptional and his first eight applications for a writ of error to the Texas Supreme Court were granted. It didn't hurt that he had clerked for Chief Justice James Patterson Alexander of the Texas Supreme Court for one or two years after law school or taken courses from him at Baylor Law School.

Before I turn to dating, the final stop on this chronicle which will segue into my courtship of Nancy Davis Labastida, my final love interest and partner, I have a few other stops to make. Mother was a big believer in joining clubs and signed me up for Cub Scouts, and in time I enrolled as a Boy Scout. In Cubs, I learned to make neckerchief slides and a few other things in a workshop in the garage of the den mother. Strangely, around this time, I also became fascinated with lassos and bullwhips, especially bullwhips—neither a part of the scouting agenda. An older scout named Jock Y–, maybe a ninth grader, was proficient in leather work, an actual scout merit badge, and was able to make long, impressive bullwhips. Jock could also crack those whips with the greatest of ease and with unbelievable marksmanship, taking on five-cent Fritos bags scattered about our den mother's backyard. I had already admired the whipsmanship of Whip Wilson, Lash Larue, and Zorro and coveted having a fine, long whip myself. The last two whipsmen wore all black outfits, which I thought was a good look for a man with a whip. Mother and Father had, on one occasion, brought me back an inexpensive souvenir whip from Mexico, but I was always eager to replace it with a by-God serious whip. The gift whip was a short whip made with inferior materials and inferior workmanship. I longed for a fine whip like the ones Jock made, until many years later I bought one from a whipmaker out of Oklahoma who delivered it personally to my law office in Dallas wearing a western shirt and boots. I still have that whip, but I need to buy some new poppers for it.

My interest in whips and learning how to crack them, not a skill a young man needed to succeed in school or to rise in Dallas society, did have one positive result from Mother's point of view, namely, fostering my friendly interest in Jock's younger sister Arleta Y–, a cute, blonde, elementary school classmate of mine. While at Arleta's house one day, on one of my rare visits to girls' houses, Arleta had an intriguing idea. She suggested that we borrow one of Jock's prize homemade whips—she knew I was into whips—a whip at least twenty feet in length, maybe twenty-five feet. Jock could make some very long whips, which took a lot of skill and muscle to crack. Her idea was to take one of Jock's prize whips and walk over to a creek in Curtis Park near the school and just have some fun. I'm not sure how the whip figured into her plan for fun other than to let me play with Jock's whip for a while; I definitely would have been up for that.

So, we walked to the park and to the creek's edge which lay below a steep, slippery bank of rock tapering down to the creek. Arleta, after putting the whip down in the grass above the creek, carefully climbed down to the water's edge. I stayed above watching Arleta cautiously making her descent. She had hardly gotten to the creek bed when suddenly Jock appeared out of nowhere above Arleta with the whip in his hand, demanding an explanation from her, and thereafter menacing her with his whip as she attempted to scramble back up the creek bank. Crack went the whip over and over on the rocky creek bank all around her fingers as Arleta struggled to climb back up while avoiding Jock's stinging whiplash. He was an excellent marksman with his whip from practicing with those Fritos sacks, and I watched in fear for Arleta as Jock did his best to scare his younger sister. He had apparently returned home, counted his whips, found one was missing, and concluded correctly that Arleta was the guilty party. I don't know how he knew to walk to Curtis Park to look for her. I didn't attempt to intervene between Jock's whip and Arleta for several reasons: one being I didn't have a whip myself to defend myself or Arleta, and two, the situation was all over in a minute or two, with no harm done to Arleta. That experience could have led to some nice experiences between Arleta and myself, except I wasn't really into dating until I got to college, and even then, not often. Then, too, maybe Arleta thought I should have intervened, even though her big brother was armed, and I was not.

My interest in lassoing and roping mentioned above was pursued by roping or yanking dining room chairs, my brother, and my sister in the house, or objects outside in the yard, as well as attempting rope tricks. My rope trick heroes were Will Rogers, Sr. and Will Rogers, Jr., who both did incredible things with their lassos. Neither Mother nor Father knew anything about roping, and neither had a lasso, and there were no roping or rope trick specialists living near us to teach me what I would have liked to know. I'm sure I could have gotten a lot better with a lasso had a teacher been available. To my interest in lassos and whips, in another ten years I added an interest in crossbows, buying a crossbow at Cullum & Boren's and practicing shooting crossbow darts into a phone book I set up in a chair in my apartment. Cullum & Boren was my go-to store for all my bow and arrow needs, and I had previously purchased a green fiberglass bow there. I was amazed that the crossbow was so powerful it could shoot a dart completely out of sight, as contrasted with my fiberglass bow and arrows.

As to my time spent in Boy Scouts, acquiring a few manly outdoor skills would have been a good way to add a little more polish to a guy who mostly stayed indoors except when playing tennis or touch football, marching in the band, playing capture the flag, catching fireflies in the summer, or playing with my whip or lasso. Although I was not a total wash-out as a Boy Scout, most of my potential for becoming an accomplished woodsman able to survive in the wilderness with only a canteen, five matches, and a Boy Scout knife remained untapped. I never got interested in lighting fires, identifying native trees and shrubs, taking long hikes to nowhere, freezing in an overnight sleeping bag on hard ground, or searching the sky for constellations (the stars would always be there, so what's the hurry?). I did earn at least six merit badges, including for art and photography (the only ones I remember for sure) and which qualified me for the Star rank. That was still fifteen badges below what was required for the Eagle rank. I forever trailed way behind the Eagle and never really got close to the Eagle rank.

Overall, Scouts had its moments with overnight campouts, singalongs ("Oh, my name is McNamara and I'm the leader of the band...," which I liked, and "Sipping Cider through a Straw," which I never liked) and the trips to New Orleans, Louisiana, and Valley Forge, Pennsylvania. However, because of my limited interest and commensurate slow progress in rank, I was increasingly outranked by scouts several years younger and shorter. These young scouts boastfully sporting their Life badges (a notch above Star) were fired up to rise in rank toward Eagle status and the prestige which came with rank. One of the other songs we inevitably sang around the campfire was "Trail the Eagle" to the tune of "On Wisconsin," a tuneful melody I hum often even now. So, all the new scouts were educated to rise from Tenderfoot (the first rank, no achievements required) through Second Class, First Class, Star, Life, and Eagle. Glad I was a scout but not bragging about it. I do want to put on record that I was able to avoid passing through a beltline, the gauntlet Scouts had to run through if caught misbehaving, like sassing the Scoutmaster. The other scouts formed the gauntlet, removing their scout belts to whack the miscreant with as he hot footed it through the gauntlet, enduring countless whacks from the double line of scouts, a line on each side. In *The Last of the Mohicans,* somebody had to survive the gauntlet—I think it may have been Uncas, one of the "good" Indians. That would have been way worse than the belt line since the Indians were holding tomahawks.

Since I have finished the subject of Scouts, a predominantly outdoor activity where my interest was tepid to lukewarm, I might as well address tennis and golf. My interest in these activities or sports was much greater, although not obvious from my accomplishments. Golf first and it won't take long. Father played golf at Northwood Club. His father and brother had been enthusiastic golfers, although, of the two, only his brother would ever break 90. Father never did. When it came to my turn to play golf, I never broke 100; when I scored in the low 100s, that was really a good day. I played some rounds at Northwood with and without Father and enjoyed walking around on that course when it wasn't too hot, but my best shots were always on the practice tee and could not be duplicated on the course itself. I never felt like I was gripping the club in a comfortable, natural way and that I believe accounted for my erratic, unreliable strokes. I was completely self-taught and don't remember any lessons from the club pro or Father either, although I'm sure he must have tried to pass on whatever he knew. He would have freely admitted that physical coordination was not his thing, although outdoor exercise was always a high priority. I did and do enjoy reading stories about famous golfers and the various antics not-so-famous players have committed. Reading George Plimpton's *The Bogey Man* was my way to pursue my interest in golf. Walking around a golf course has always taken more time than I wanted to devote to that pastime.

Then there's tennis, for which I have had a lifelong interest, something short of a passion since I first started playing in grade school on public courts where players had to furnish their own nets. I liked tennis first because it doesn't take long to play a couple of sets, maybe an hour or so, and because it provided greater exercise than golf. Tennis was my father's sport and that of my grandfather and uncle before they took up golf, perhaps because they disliked running around on a hard court after having done so for so many years. Mother arranged for tennis lessons for me at Northwood from Wayne Sabin and later Armando Vieira, both retired professional players of note in their day. I remember Vieira saying the best player he ever saw was Bobby Riggs who, in his later years, was defeated in a celebrated match by Billie Jean King after Riggs had beaten Margaret Court Smith in a similar challenge match. Pro Sabin set me up to play a practice match with little Harvey Davis, who would turn out to be the oldest little brother of my future third bride, Nancy Davis Labastida. Pro Sabin said Harvey could give me a pretty good match. I soon found out that Harvey, a small guy several years younger than me, was a human backboard who could hit them back to me until I hit the ball out or into the net.

Thinking back, I suspect Sabin knew what was in store for me playing little Harvey since he knew both our games. I had a good flat first serve when it occasionally went in; Harvey had little or no zip on his serve, but it always went in, and he beat me so bad I can't remember the score. Another time, Sabin or Vieira sandbagged me by pairing me up with Mike Amis, two years older than me but at the top of the club tennis ladder hanging in the tennis shack. Mike and I went out to hit some balls, and he toyed with me by throwing up three balls simultaneously on his serve and hitting one of them. I must say I felt disrespected by this maneuver which created confusion on my part and represented obvious trickery—possibly against the rules, certainly against the spirit of a game in which everyone wore white. He was on SMU's tennis team and should not have been paired with me. Sabin was probably chuckling as he watched me play stronger players through the shack window.

At college I wasn't good enough to play on the Baylor tennis team and just found miscellaneous partners in the dorm to hit with. One day I was watching Baylor's team play a visiting team from another Texas school. When one of the Baylor players didn't show up for the match, tennis coach Bob, who was also my PE coach in tennis, spied me over in the stands and said, "*Guittard*, get ready to go in." I didn't know whether he was joking or not, but the moment passed somehow, and I did not have to go in, and the Baylor team was able to press on without me. Whew, that was close! That would have been really embarrassing.

My best moment with a Jack Kramer racket in my hand occurred ten or more years later when I played Steve Lanfer, a visiting friend of my roommate Bill Hallman, both Stanford graduates. Steve might as well have been a player on Stanford's tennis team. That day I was playing way above my skill level and was able to get a couple of games off Steve in both sets before he closed them out with his much stronger game. In the years that followed I never played that well again but fed my appetite for tennis by watching touring pros when they came to town. One afternoon I saw a battle of tennis titans of the past and former world number ones: Pancho Gonzales, in a long five-set match, defeated Ken Rosewall. Pancho's wife, the very tan Miss Rheingold of 1958, was in the stands watching her husband struggle through maybe seventy or more games in the five-set, almost endless match they played on a very hot Dallas day. In one set, the score was 14-12. There was no tie-breaker rule in the 60s and 70s. After it was all over, an exhausted but victorious Pancho, dripping with sweat from head to toe, took off his shoes, peeled off his socks, and hobbled barefoot back to the club locker room. On another day, I was able to see tennis legends Billie Jean King play Margaret Court Smith on a special indoor court near Northwood Club built by H.L. Hunt's son-in-law Al Hill. I don't remember who won, only that my neighbor Dick Sartain spilled his Pepsi on his seat before we left to go home. Dick happened to be sitting that day in the special seat of one of H.L. Hunt's daughters, Margaret Hunt Hill, who was married to Al Hill and was not present that day.

Finally, before going into Mother's final efforts to produce a well-turned-out and datable son ready to cut a swath through Dallas single women and break the hearts of the daughters of Mother's club friends, I will address Father's efforts to teach or polish me, topic by topic:

Posture: "Straighten up, shoulders back, and don't hunch over as you walk. You look like you're about to tip over." I gradually corrected this.

Mouth position: "Unless you are eating or talking, keep it closed." Father thought walking hunched forward with my mouth slack-jawed was a bad look. I think I finally corrected the mouth position.

Reading: "You should be reading all the time. I always had a book in my hand when I was growing up. You should also." Despite the advice, I didn't start really reading much until college.

Writing: "Draft your essays and then revise them until you get it right; don't hand in sloppy work. Delete all unnecessary words." I started carefully drafting and revising my written work in a college philosophy class in ethics. Surprisingly, my English literature courses didn't require much writing.

Calisthenics: "Do push-ups to build your pecs and sit-ups to flatten your belly. Walk for exercise." I did this on a random basis, which was not very often.

Geography: "Learn the names and locations of the world's cities and that of rivers and mountain ranges—you will need that to understand history." The only time I tried to do this was for a few weeks under Father's prodding when I lived with my parents. I don't think I even had an atlas when studying history at college. The problem for me with geography and with history was that there was too much to know to even begin to understand either subject. That's a flimsy excuse, I know, but I was thoroughly intimidated by the vast quantity of information in both subjects—impossible for any normal human to master. I must admit, though, that Father did seem to have a deep grasp of both subjects. But his father was, after all, a history professor.

Moral outlook: "Avoid thinking solely about yourself. Thinking about others will cure your self-consciousness. People will hold any show of egotism against you. That's what happened to Billy Boastful (a well-known Texas attorney and politician who, in my father's opinion, flamed out with the electorate or his political party with his boastfulness). Stand up for the right principles, don't hang back waiting for others to speak." Seems like there have been a few times I've done okay on this one.

Timidity: "Push yourself to reach out to others. Say hello, offer to shake their hands, begin the conversation, and take the initiative. The other person may be shier than you and will be happy you did." Father exhorted me while at Baylor to go by and chat with some of the Baylor faculty he had known during his college days, including Mrs. Armstrong, wife and partner of the legendary Professor A.J. Armstrong. I know I should have, and she would have been happy to see me, but I never did. Good advice, though. In later years, I did make substantial progress in this area, although one lawyer colleague would say of me decades later, "Charles is the kind of guy who sneaks up on you from the front."

Dating: "Girls would welcome some interest from you. [Regarding a train trip to an annual bar association meeting in California] One of my law partners will be taking along his cute daughter Suzy R–. You might pay some attention to her on the train ride." A good idea, but I would not be ready to pay attention to Suzy for another fifteen years, when we had one date to a steak restaurant.

Sex: "Avoid sex before marriage. If you ever give in, it will be that much easier the next time. Sex before marriage will lead to a whited sepulcher sooner or later." Father did not elaborate on the meaning of the term "whited sepulcher." It sounded really bad, and I was afraid to ask him to clarify. In looking back, his advice seems to have been his attempt, at least in part, to inoculate me against the "young man's damsel in distress disease," so vividly portrayed in W. Somerset Maugham's *Of Human Bondage*, in which a young doctor is enmeshed with a promiscuous waitress who develops syphilis. Father's advice foreshadowed a sermon warning against the power of lust by my Southern Baptist pastor years later. Dr. Herbert R. Howard declared in a grave tone from the pulpit of Park Cities Baptist Church that one day he was standing on the street corner near the Greyhound bus station in downtown Dallas waiting for the light. At that moment, as an unusually attractive woman began walking across the street in front of Dr. Howard, a man standing next to him mused aloud, "I'd spend a thousand years in hell for one night with her." The metaphor, although arguably scary to some in a mostly married congregation sitting in comfortable pews, made it almost sound, at least to a relatively inexperienced young buck like myself, as if sex before marriage with a gorgeous libertine might be so exciting as to be worth the risk, consequences be damned.

Sex, a postscript: As curious and extreme as the above advice from Father may seem to our modern ears, Mother would not have been up for giving any advice at all on this subject, having received little or no instruction herself from her mother before leaving on her honeymoon with Father.

Religion: Father was Christian but made few pronouncements as to particular creeds or essential beliefs. He was a regular attendee of Sunday services and of a couples' class with Mother. He also taught Sunday school from time to time. One Sunday he worked in a reference to the comic strip character Alley Oop to lighten up the lesson for that day. Another strip Father read but I didn't was *Pogo*, which was always political, even more so than *Little Abner*. Reading the comic strips on Sundays always pepped up Sundays for me and put me in a good mood before listening later to a dour preacher drone on at the eleven o'clock hour. Ultimately, I concluded that Father's ideas on the nature of the Christian faith reflected more thinking than most seminary-trained preachers exhibited.

Careers: Father was an appellate attorney who became a trial judge and then an appellate judge. In semi-retirement, he served as a mediator of litigated disputes, by court appointment or by agreement of the parties. He did not lean on his children to pursue a legal career, although he did not oppose such a move. As a trial court judge, his forte among others was asking penetrating questions to the attorneys in court before him, such as: "Mr. Smith, do you agree with Justice McDonald's argument in the concurring opinion that...?" In chambers, he was particularly famous for referring to hundreds of his hand-written 3x5 cards in his desk drawer that summarized the decisions of the Texas courts which might be relevant to the case before him. He based his summaries on his review of the advance sheets he received from the opinions' publisher.

So if, as previously mentioned, the intended crown jewels down the road of polishing efforts by Mother and Father were my marriage and a family, what were the more immediate results they may have secretly hoped for? Obviously, they hoped their efforts would be successful to the fullest extent in every area. Mother perhaps would have been extremely pleased if her firstborn son had decided to join a men's social club and then, with enviable aplomb, cut a broad swath through the marriageable daughters of her Dallas club friends, perhaps unavoidably breaking a few hearts along the way. And what aspirations did Father entertain for me? A well-rounded scholar-athlete with a tennis racket in one hand and *The Rise and Fall of the Roman Empire* in the other? Perhaps a reincarnation of "Whizzer" White or Pete Dawkins? Or perhaps one who could draw freehand a map of Europe with all the important cities and rivers noted and could do twenty push-ups and fifteen squat-jumps before breakfast? We will never know the answers to those questions, but hopefully, when Mother and Father see the final report card at the end of this piece, they will sign it and at least say to themselves, "Well, not bad. Not really bad at all."

PART III

Mother's Conscientiousness in Health Matters, Including Complexion and Teeth

There are several more topics we need to address before opening the vital topic of dating, including the teenage scourges of acne and crooked teeth. Mother inherited her interest in health and doctors from her father, Dr. John Lester Kee, who was by all accounts a conscientious and knowledgeable Waco physician. Family tradition has it that Dr. Kee made the high mark on the 1916 medical boards. Consequently, in matters of her children's health, Mother was super proactive. When our noses were stopped up, our ears hurt, or our foreheads a little warm, she would fly to our bedsides with stoppers of nose drops, ear drops, cold rags, or thermometers. When we had a little fever, chicken pox, mumps, or measles, or were nauseated or had diarrhea, she would bring whatever food and medicine was needed: crackers and 7-Up, Jell-O, chicken and noodle soup, and medicines like paregoric, Kaopectate, calamine lotion, cod liver oil, and other standard over-the-counter medications. Because at home we had no television until the mid-1950s, I would while away the morning hours cooped up with a fever listening to Don McNeill's *Breakfast Club*, *The Arthur Godfrey Show* with various Julius LaRosa songs, The Stamps Quartet Broadcast which often featured "Give the World a Smile," or to radio melodramas like *Helen Trent* or *Our Gal Sunday*, which came on right after *Helen Trent*. It was all pretty lame fare for a young boy who wasn't yet much into reading, and it didn't compare to nighttime programs like *The Lone Ranger*, *The Shadow*, and *Gunsmoke*. I would much rather have been outside playing with my whip or my lasso or my bow and arrows.

It was always a crisis, however, when it was time to get one of the usual rounds of shots (tetanus, typhoid, whooping cough, diphtheria, or polio) children were supposed to have. There was always a lot of crying on the drive to the pediatrician's office—"Please, Mother, do we have to? Again? We were here last year!" Once there, we were quickly ushered into the "shot room," which strongly smelled of medicinal alcohol and where the crying-hardened shot nurses hung out. One in particular was a rough, no-nonsense kind of nurse with frizzy blonde hair that needed brushing and who looked like she may have served in a military hospital somewhere tending to soldiers trying to avoid the rigors of basic training. Nurse Stern's shots always seemed to hurt more. The other nurse had better hair, was a brunette, and had a kindlier manner and administered shots that didn't hurt as much, but we were never asked which nurse we preferred to give us our shots. The faces of both nurses are burned in my memory. They didn't give out lollipops either—that would have been for wimps. However, I was a wimp and would have liked a lollipop to distract me from my sore arm.

A decade later, when Mother was advised I needed some shots before a European trip with other college kids, she asked my grandfather, Dr. Kee, conveniently located on the seventh floor of the Amicable Building in Waco, to give me my required pre-trip inoculations, one of which was for tetanus (lockjaw). I showed up at his office on the seventh floor for my shot in 1963, but someone got mixed up—maybe my grandfather, even though he still had his marbles—and I apparently received a shot sometimes confused with the standard pre-trip tetanus shot called "horse serum" or "tetanus anti-toxin." The result, within a matter of hours, was to freakishly enlarge my earlobes, lips, and the tip of my nose, as well as make my knees hurt when I tried to walk. I should have had someone take a picture of me. I stayed away from class for about a week and didn't show my face to anyone, including girls. That may have been the week I got behind in a German class that met five times a week, and I had to force myself to return to class. Anyway, after two weeks, I was more or less back to normal, but I wonder to this day how I got the wrong shot.

Now for those inevitable health topics: acne and crooked teeth. Both Mother and Father had a hand in dealing with my acne. I had off-and-on issues with acne through high school, most of college, and law school, a relatively mild case by some standards, but disturbing to me, nonetheless. Father's advice, while usually sensitive and carefully worded in most (but not all) other matters, was heavy-handed on this issue, and, like the metaphor of the whited sepulcher, once I had heard it, it was impossible to erase from my mind. Father confided that he too had had a case of acne himself as a young man, and one day my Guittard grandfather thought he could scare Father from putting his hands on his face by saying: "Have you ever walked behind a horse as it has a bowel movement and noticed the way its anus turns itself inside out after it is finished and made you want to puke? That's the way you look after you've laid your hands on your face." In his partial defense, my grandfather Frank Guittard grew up on a farm in Ohio and knew what he was talking about. Father repeated the story to me, hoping the shock value would have a beneficial effect on my complexion. However, it made me more self-conscious than ever, which was counter-productive considering his cure for my shyness noted earlier. Sometimes "scaring them straight" is not the way to go in giving advice to children, or in church sermons either.

Mother's approach to my skin problem was more scientific. She took me to a downtown dermatologist in the Medical Arts Building which was razed for low occupancy rates forty-six years ago. After I was seated in the special chair where all torturees were expected to sit, Dr. Strangways would take a piece of gauze, pick up a piece of dry ice with it so as not to burn his precious fingers, dip it in acetone, and then go over my face, burning off one or more layers of skin bearing traces of acne. I had several such treatments always making my face beet red. If you remember the scene in the *Phantom of the Opera* right after acid is thrown in Claude Rains' face or Lon Chaney's face, that will give you a taste of my experience, just more intense than mine. After concluding the series of treatments over a period of weeks, we said goodbye to Dr. Strangways, but I still had outbreaks of acne from time to time, despite my hours in Dr. Strangways' chair.

Now I was in college, on my own to deal with the problem, and definitely interested in dating. My approach to my skin problem, developed from reading and experimentation, was two-fold: first, reduce my intake of sweets, especially chocolate pie and Sara Lee pound cake; second, get plenty of sun; if I couldn't take enough time to spend in the sun, then I would use a sun lamp to produce a healthy sunburn on my face. The operative theory going around, at least around in my head, was that acne was caused by excessive oil in the skin somehow (the evidence seemed to be anecdotal only) caused by eating rich foods. So, I tried reducing sweets and it may have helped a little, but I was never sure. The sun lamp treatments also may have helped, but on occasion had adverse consequences, such as producing large clear blisters on my cheeks and chin which had a way of oozing fluid. Suffice it to say, on the days my sun lamp treatment had gone wrong, I was reluctant to go out in public. On one or more occasions, the error was actually mine as I, after skillfully positioning the lamp and carefully placing wetted pieces of cotton over my eyes, had usually dosed off under the ultraviolet rays and lost track of time. I would wake up after thirty-five minutes instead of fifteen or twenty. I don't know why I didn't use my alarm clock and just relied on checking my wristwatch.

Mother did definitely find a solution for my teeth problem—too many teeth taking up too much room with permanent teeth waiting in the wings anxious to make their appearance—and found first a dentist and then an orthodontist. The dentist removed ten tenacious baby teeth in one session, which went under my pillow that night and were replaced before dawn by ten dimes from the tooth fairy. After that, I removed another baby tooth or two myself by wiggling them or trying a Rube Goldberg technique: tying the tooth to a string and the other end of the string to a doorknob and then quickly slamming the door. That was not recommended by any professionals in the yellow pages and resulted in chipping one of my brother's permanent teeth after he tired of wiggling a baby tooth with his finger. I don't know who showed us the door technique which would have been impractical for my ten baby teeth. On one of my next trips to the dentist, in one fell swoop, he removed three wisdom teeth (permanent teeth!) to make room for other permanent teeth troublemakers. At that point, all went well until it became obvious that my remaining permanent teeth did not have the slightest idea about how to line up with each other, and certain top and bottom teeth in the front started surging forward while others were falling back.

So now Mother found a convenient orthodontist in our neighborhood shopping center to introduce me to braces—metal bands and tight wires on every tooth in my head with rubber bands later to pull the teeth into position. Appointments were scheduled every two weeks. Just as my teeth started recovering from the tightening two weeks prior, I would be dropped off at the orthodontist, Dr. Hurt—I'm positive he was a borderline sadist—to tighten the wires once again. I know it is unfair to say he was a sadist except that he never liked me groaning when it hurt and seemed to be disgusted with my responses. Somehow, Laurence Olivier as a Nazi war criminal with access to dentist instruments comes to mind, Olivier working on Dustin Hoffman in *The Marathon Man*. That is, if you want to understand a patient's experience in an orthodontist's chair. The other consequence of the "no pain, no gain" orthodontist work was that I couldn't play my trombone full out in band practice for several days until my teeth, gums, and nerves recovered. Not that I was that great a trombone player, but my tone was always fuzzier when my braces were newly tightened, affecting my embouchure. Aiming for a bright clear tone was always my ambition as a trombonist, a goal always beyond the grasp of my embouchure.

The final phase in rejiggering the positions of my teeth was wearing retainers, first a thin plastic flesh-colored appliance to wear during the day, and then later a black rubber retainer to wear at night to prevent teeth from returning to their prior positions. Wearing the black rubber retainer was a piece of cake, although it always fell out of my mouth about as soon as I dozed off. In later years, I saved that black retainer in its little plastic container for no good reason—maybe I thought all my grandchildren would surround me one day demanding to hear my teeth straightening stories and I would have that retainer to show and awe them with. I like props when I tell stories. Overall, the straightening of my teeth was mostly successful, so thanks, Mother, for keeping me from being a snaggle-toothed eighty-year-old, or college student, for that matter. In fairness, I would add that in the last ten years or so, some of the teeth we thought were "straightened" are now trying to return to their starting positions. I guess they have minds of their own.

One final note on Mother's interest in my health. When I was a college student, my uncle John L. Kee, Jr., an MD like his father, suggested I go to Boston to be checked over by a well-known Boston cardiologist named Dera Kinsey, and Mother went with me. I suppose she toured Boston during the day while doctors x-rayed, drew blood, took my blood pressure, and poked and prodded me for about a week. I have no idea what she did with her time, but she always dropped me off at the appointed hour in the morning and picked me up promptly in the afternoon. The real upside to the trip was there was an attractive young brunette nurse on my ward at Massachusetts Memorial who was several years older than I. That made my days at the hospital less tedious. After I was discharged, I wrote her a letter in care of the hospital—I don't remember exactly what the letter said, but it was probably bordering on mildly flirtatious—and mailed it. I received a nice response within a week or so from this young nurse, thanking me for writing, but making it crystal clear my letter was the sort that young nurses sometimes receive from young male patients after their discharges. In closing, she wished me and my health well, over and out. I did not follow up on her letter.

PART IV

Dating—What I Learned on My Own About Calling a Girl and Getting a Date, Preparing for a Date, and Getting the Second Date

Since the reader may be about to give up on hearing about how my parents encouraged me to date girls and how they may have helped me, I will cover that right now, and it won't take too long. First, all the polishings already described were preparation for, and related to, meeting and dating young women. Mother, as mentioned above, considered marriage and family the crown jewels of her plans for her children. As crown jewels go, I would rank those pretty high myself, although not exclusive of other worthy goals of this day like watching CNN, *Dateline*, *Wheel of Fortune*, and an occasional *Hoarders*. There may be some irony in the fact that of the three children polished by my parents, only your author, with a case of self-consciousness and recurrent skin problems, was able to find three partners who would consent to marry him, fathered three children, and grandfathered four. The polish added or encouraged by my parents—table manners, piano and art lessons, dancing lessons, playing in the band and orchestra, Cub Scouts and Boy Scouts, learning to play bridge, training in speech, debating in high school and college, playing a good game of tennis, and addressing skin and teeth problems—all played a part in readying me for the game of dating and finding a spouse (or spouses) on a much larger stage in my late twenties, mid-forties, and late seventies.

Eventually, I was obviously on my own, away at Baylor, or out of Dallas, free of parental admonitions and overview, and ready to play the dating game. Mother had effectively vetoed my idea of playing in the Baylor band at college because she felt I would just end up hanging around my band buddies and ignoring the girls, i.e., like in high school. So, when I went to Baylor, and for the most part not having band buddies, I just hung around my bridge and debate buddies and ignored the girls. And my go for pizza and ice cream buddies. Frankly, being around the girls in the Baylor band— assuming I could have passed a band audition and gotten in the band, which was not a given as Baylor had a really good band and I was only a 2d chair trombonist in a high school band—would have been a good thing. Band girls and I would have had a common interest, and I would have been exposed to them at all our practice sessions, plus riding on the bus to football games. That would have helped to warm things up with a few of them. As it was, I had a handful of dates, mostly blind dates with a few girls either at college or during summer breaks, and I didn't have a real interest in any of them. Of course, I noticed the campus beauties featured in the yearbooks at year's end, but I had no classes with them or other contacts. I thought about writing a letter to one of the gorgeous campus beauties who didn't know me from Adam's Off Ox, but I thought better of it and didn't. Sunday school would have been a good place to meet a girl from Waco or Baylor, although I never really connected with a class or teacher that I liked (my excuse), and only attended on a handful of Sundays. I opted instead to go to eleven o'clock church service at First Baptist Waco with my maternal grandparents and then to lunch with them on their dime at Sam Coates, a popular Waco restaurant on Highway 6 "Where Good Food Speaks for Itself." The Sam Coates Restaurant was owned by a Baylor graduate by that name who had played on one of Baylor's championship football teams in the early 1920s glory years and featured a famous Black Bottom Pie. Not an easy choice— meeting girls at Sunday school or chowing down on free food and Black Bottom Pie.

Mother did encourage me to go on a month-long trip to Europe (the one I had to get shots for), which included twelve days on the S.S. United States and S.S. France ocean liners. That was a good idea—one of her best—and a great trip. In Florence, Italy, I invited an attractive and very classy Sophie Newcomb student, who was the most interesting to me among the twenty-five girls in our group, to the opera. The opera, Donizetti's *Lucia di Lammermoor*, wherein several characters die tragically and Lucia flips out in her famous mad scene, was great and we had a good time. However, my date had a boyfriend back home, probably a fiancé, and my interest was cut off at the pass.

What I learned from Mother's polishing may be obvious to all, but a guy can be burnished to a fare-thee-well by well-meaning parents and that is all well and good, but that by itself won't necessarily get him to pick up the telephone to call a girl. Here is what I have learned, totally on my own, regarding calling up a girl:

1. Pick someone who you would really like to know better or, in the alternative, someone you may not know very well but want to spend a little time with as an experiment. The girl should be able to place you somehow, so you don't have to spend time explaining where you met or saw each other. If you have never met, you may have to meet for coffee first, but I have never had that kind of date, and perhaps it should be avoided if you have the option.

2. Write her name and telephone number down legibly on a pad of paper. This is very important. You don't want to stumble calling her name or calling her by the wrong name, including the name of another girl if you have several girls in mind or written on your pad of paper.

3. If you want to increase your odds of getting an affirmative response on the day you have finally screwed your courage to the sticking place as advised by motivation expert Lady Macbeth, write down the names and numbers of more than one likely girl. That way, a potential turn-down from the first girl won't be as devastating. And, having a backup plan, you will feel more confident with the first girl you call. Admission: I probably did not have a backup plan that

many times and so was always anxious about calling a girl.

4. Plan out what you are going to say in advance. If you barely know a girl, hopefully she will remember you somehow, some way, such as being in a class at school, not as a shy lurker who was always staring at her.

5. Don't try shooting the breeze with them over the telephone unless you have the gift of gabbing with girls you don't know. Never my thing. Just propose the date and bring the call to a conclusion after reaching an agreement on the details. Then, you will have a little ego boost for the rest of the day.

6. Typically, I would write down the name of the movie or play, or a football game I would be offering to take them to and when I might pick them up, leaving time to grab a bite to eat. Visiting over a meal in advance is a good idea so that the rest of the evening won't be as awkward. Also, let them know, if you think it would be helpful, what kind of clothes you will be wearing and answer any questions she may ask. As to whether you should avoid certain kinds of entertainments or activities, you might avoid miniature golf and bowling. I had a dull date to play miniature golf one time, but it might work for you.

7. It is crucial that once your fingers have touched the telephone to make your call and have actually picked up the receiver, you must force yourself to dial the number and carry on until you hear her voice. Then, under no circumstances should you dial her number and then hang up after hearing her say, "Hello...," since that failure may create a phone phobia you will have to overcome the next time.

8. Once you have lined up the date and answered any questions, say goodbye and any other friendly words of closure, and hang up. Do not call back before the date to chat unless you have a very good reason to do so, like suggesting she bring an umbrella, her bathing suit, or whatever. Actually, I'm stretching it here as I have never had a swimming date.

Now that you and the girl you called have agreed on the details of a date, you will want to prepare yourself for the date. I don't mean taking a shower, wearing suitable clothes, spraying your breath, and flossing, combing your hair and shaving, and the sort of things that all go without saying. I mean tooling your brain and tongue for conversation with your date, conversation that will keep her interested in chatting with you. I recommend the following:

1. Try to think of something interesting to say if you can, but don't stress out on this. The main thing is just to get a conversation started, however trite, and then you and your date can gradually get it going in a more compelling direction. If you and your date can't get a conversation going, you and she are probably not a good match anyway.

2. On a pocket-sized notepad, write down some keywords that will trigger a few topics for conversation that might also interest the girl.

3. Study those notes at home before leaving for the date and say the keywords to yourself several times without looking back at the paper.

4. On the car ride over to pick her up at her residence, at stop-lighted intersections, glance over at your notepad on the seat beside you to remind yourself of the keywords.

5. Once on your date, if the conversation is going well without checking your notes, that's fine. You are

home free. If it is not, on your first bathroom trip, you can pull out your notes for a quick review.

6. My experience with notes generally is that once I felt the self confidence that always came from having ready access to them in my pocket, I rarely even brought up the topics on my notepad. Just having them handy was all I needed.

7. I used to prepare notes from almost the beginning of my dating up through meeting my second wife. I did not need notes for my first in-person date with my third wife, Nancy, but I'm confident I made notes for some of our early conversations, texts, and emails. These would add up to hundreds of such contacts before meeting her in person in Austin, Texas, in September 2021, twelve days after our first contact online.

8. At the conclusion of the first date, my recommend-ation for self-conscious men who become unduly anxious thinking about picking up the telephone and making plans for a second date is simple. At the end of the first date, propose a second date a week or two away, what kind of date you are proposing, when you will pick her up, etc. Have the details of a possible second date in mind before putting the gearshift in drive for the first date. I have no advice on kissing (on the lips, not the forehead) a girl you hardly know on the first date. Although it seems harmless, you have to play that by ear, and it will depend on whether it feels appropriate.

PART V

The Final Report Card on the Parental Polishing, Marrying Out of My League, And the Moral of the Story

Before detailing the scores on the final report card, some early returns on parental polishing. Mother had friends with Party Service in Dallas, which arranged escorts for former debutantes. Receiving such an invitation with a girl's name on a little card, I would be directed to call the girl and arrange to escort her to a debutante function at a country club. On one occasion, I picked up former deb Betty and we chatted on the way to the event. After we were seated with our punch and cookies, a tall special male friend of hers—had to have been 6 foot 10—sat down next to her on the other side and started chatting her up, mostly out of my hearing. I did hear her saucily whisper to him, "I wish we were here under different circumstances." I had one other Party Service arranged date with a Veronica, again a former deb, one so quiet and reserved I could see why her parents had wanted her to "turn her out" to Dallas society. In neither case, despite all the polishing efforts described elsewhere, did either girl show any interest in me or did we have a second date. Both occasions were during my early days as a new lawyer in Dallas in the late 1960s when I was just trying to find my bearings.

If only those two experiences are considered, one would have to conclude that the jury was still out on how well I had been polished. It might have helped had I been a member of one of the men's social clubs like Dervish or Calyx. One of my older Guittard cousins—who was truly a dashing attorney about town and a former high school football player—and his roommates had been members of the Dervish Club and reportedly had a great time taking Dallas' fairest all-around Dallas. However, if one takes a long look at my polishing, both from my parents and what I learned on my own from the 1960s (when I was in my twenties) through the early 2020s (when I was almost eighty), the final picture is thankfully more positive. Naturally, that's the one reflected in the scorecard below.

Here are the grade categories in which I have graded the cumulative effect of parental polishing and my own efforts:

S for efforts deemed successful

M for efforts deemed moderately successful

N for efforts deemed to have no lasting impact or deficient

O for minimal efforts or skills learned basically on my own

In alphabetical order:

S Bridge skills

N Calisthenics

S Career advice (by example only)

S Dancing skills

O Dating skills (learned on my own)

S Debating skills

N Geography skills

S Health matters generally

S Health matters—complexion

S Health matters—teeth

S Manners

S Mouth position

S Moral outlook

S Music Appreciation

N Outdoor skills

M Posture

S Public speaking

M at first, then S—Reading

S Religious training

N or O, take your pick—Sex education learned on my own

M at first, then S—Timidity. Progress took most of my life

Overall grade by today's standards: Let's give me an S minus, the only seriously lacking scores being in dating and sex education. In these categories, the lower scores were likely a result of my parents' limited education on these topics and the difficulty of their generation in talking about them. Certain other areas don't get an S or M, but that was not for Mother or Father's lack of trying.

———— ·◦◣◥◦· ————

Now we are ready to talk briefly about Nancy and my third marriage. Very soon in this volume, I will go into this subject much more in detail in *"Wow, It's Almost Like We Walked Hand In Hand through Our Childhood!" A Memoir of a Third Courtship & December Marriage that Wasted No Time.* Both our families were stunned at these developments and brothers on both sides wanted to put their reactions on record. My brother on learning that I was planning to marry Nancy Davis Labastida, an attractive and world-traveled widow just off a half-century marriage to a distinguished bilingual attorney with a long career at the U.N., announced that I was marrying "out of my league," or maybe he said, *way* out of my league." Thanks, John, for that non-boost. Perhaps one or more of Nancy's brothers was of the same view, as one of them called an emergency Zoom meeting to discuss the matter with Nancy's siblings and let them weigh in on this weighty matter. For this meeting, to which I was not invited and felt anxious, I prepared a one-page handout marketing myself to her family. That may sound weird, but that's what I did. One of Nancy's brothers did not oppose the marriage but withheld judgment, saying that he would need five references from me in addition to the written summary. That request for references may have been offered in jest, but I didn't really know Nancy's family at the time or what to make of the request, so thanks, Clayton, for your non-boost. Ultimately, I was able to laugh off the request for references as I felt pretty confident I was on solid ground with Nancy. Anyway, I damn sure wasn't going to furnish any references. Heck, I was retired from that sort of thing. And after all, I had no loony ex-girlfriends in the background pinning scary messages on my door, my used model car was in good shape and showed no trace of collision, and I've already mentioned that I had previously been able to persuade two other marriageable women to marry me. No turn downs at all. After all, if Nancy wanted me and there was resistance from her family, she would just have to fight for me. Of course, she was already behind our marriage project, so I calmed down, and we exited the family approval gauntlet without further hiccups.

So how and when did Nancy first pop up on my radar screen? I became aware of Nancy first in August 2021 when Classmates.com sent me an automated message asking if I knew her and, if so, what I thought of her, encouraging me to pick some adjectives (I picked "athletic" and "attractive") from a list of a hundred words or so. Classmates.com routinely sends members information regarding people graduating from the same high school, as long as the classes didn't graduate too far apart. I knew of Nancy Davis Labastida only because of her photos as a star player on Hillcrest's tennis team in the 1957 Hillcrest High School yearbook (*The Panther*). I had never met her or seen her at Northwood Club, where our families had been members.

Although I did not really know Nancy when Classmates.com contacted me, we had a lot in common. I had played tennis at Northwood often and was aware of her tennis-playing family, including her father, Harvey L. Davis; her sister Virginia; and her brother little Harvey; all of whom I saw playing on the Northwood courts. Although I had stopped playing tennis years before meeting Nancy, I still had my beat-up, ancient Jack Kramer wooden racket and, more importantly, my interest in tennis and tennis players. The same is true of my interest in bridge, which I would learn was an important part of Nancy's social life as well as fuel for her lifelong competitive drive. Nancy, for several reasons, had gradually given up tennis in her late seventies while keeping her own ancient, beat-up Jack Kramer racket and an armful of other more modern rackets. I had given up both bridge and tennis while maintaining an interest in both. Bridge and tennis would be, among many other connections that we had, the ones that initially drew us together as a couple. Today, my Jack Kramer racket and Nancy's Jack Kramer and other rackets hang, hers proudly, mine meekly, neatly on the wall inside the small half-bath in the utility room, where the slightest vibration can cause them to crash to the floor.

And the fact that she was and is funny, intelligent, and affectionate didn't hurt either. By the way, Nancy and I knew each so well from our emails in the fall of 2021 before I met her in person at her home that I kissed her immediately upon exiting my car. It was mutual and, there being no time to waste, we got that out of the way.

There is a MORAL to this memoir, and it is this: Unless you love to dance or are just incredibly good-looking, don't throw away your book on bridge or your old tennis racket. Mother and Father's polishing was well-intended and effective in many respects, but they got the bridge and tennis parts exactly right.

The explosion at the bridge table and its aftermath.

Jock practices whip-cracking to teach sister Arleta a lesson.

Judge Guittard counsels Charles regarding premarital sex.

Nurse Stern administers a booster shot to Charles' arm.

"Wow, it's almost like we walked hand in hand through our childhood!"

A Memoir of a Third Courtship & December Marriage That Wasted No Time

This memoir reflects the beginning of the relationship between two personalities seemingly poles apart who hit it off the moment they met. It is about a quiet guy, your author, who, in the opinion of his friends, could sneak up on you from the front, and the exuberant gal with a booming voice who, according to her family, you could hear coming around the corner. It represents a detective story in which your author, his curiosity initially engaged by automatic messages from Classmates.com, sought to find out more about this Nancy Davis Labastida, a name from sixty-five years back in the misty past. The story blossoms into a romance and then marriage in a little over one hundred days for these octogenarians. How that could happen in this age and time for a widow and a widower who had already lived long, satisfying lifetimes apart, who were very different, and for whom marriage at their age didn't follow the norm or the expectation of their peers is the question answered by this memoir.

A simplified chronology of their courtship and marriage in 2021 in Charles' words is as follows:

August 22: I received an unsolicited automated message from Classmates.com asking whether I remembered Nancy Davis Labastida and attached photos from the 1957 *Hillcrest Panther*. The photos showed Nancy with the school tennis team, which rang a bell although I didn't really remember Nancy. The message asked me to check words describing Nancy, and I checked only "athletic" and "attractive." Classmates.com, with internet speed, sent my responses to Nancy, suggesting I remembered her when technically I didn't.

August 22, 9:40 p.m.: Nancy messaged me on Facebook with the following: "Hi, Charles. Did you know my father, Professor Harvey Davis at SMU School of Law? I remember we were friends at Hillcrest [High School]."

August 23: Nancy and I were both busy messaging each other on Facebook and then emailing each other sharing memories: her memories of her victories at state tournaments at ages fourteen, sixteen, and seventeen, growing up and her father's tennis partners at Northwood Club, and my memories of great tennis matches I had watched of the top pros. Nancy closed an early message with: "I also play bridge. Since COVID, I have discovered bridge online. PS My email is: [email address has been removed for privacy]."

August 23: Later that day, after I had shared the address of my son Bob in Austin, Nancy replied: "Your son and his family live about fifteen miles from me. I live in Northwest Hills and would love to get together with you the next time you are in Austin." I replied later the same day: "Great! I will let you know the timing."

August 24-25: Nancy and I shared several emails as she checked me out.

August 27: I called Nancy for the first time, and we had an easy conversation mentioning our common tennis friends and acquaintances. She seemed to think I'm funny, and I learned that she is a humorous kind spirit who gets along well with others and likes to travel. It's obvious that things have warmed up, although we have still haven't met in person.

August 28: Nancy and I have discussed meeting each other in person in Austin, Texas. However, since my dog, Maggie, was ill and at the vet, Nancy offered to drive to Dallas. Things are moving along.

August 29: Nancy and I emailed each other several times. I worked on my book *I WILL TEACH HISTORY.*

August 30: A sad day as Maggie died at the vet with me by her side and Nancy on the phone as I sat in a little room with Maggie. Later, I worked on the book.

August 31: Started packing for my trip to Austin. Watched Djokovic play Rune at the U.S. Open. Worked on book.

September 1: Found scrapbooks and other items to show Nancy during a visit at her house. Worked on book.

September 3-6: Drove to Nancy's house in Austin. Got lost in Austin in an endless loop seemingly commanded by my GPS. Called Nancy to explain my predicament; she felt sorry for me and told me to come on to her house, where I stayed after not being able to find the La Quinta. In the morning, the first time Nancy saw me that day (around 6 a.m.) she was obviously startled, blurting out "What are you doing up?" Later that day, Nancy's sister Virginia and Bill Oliver came over for dinner; Bill brought his guitar and sang some popular songs; Virginia, Nancy, and I joined in when we knew the words. Nancy's brother Harvey and wife, Gayle, came over the next day. On Sunday, we visited my son Bob, daughter-in-law Candace, and their boys, and I then drove back to Dallas.

September 10: I traded in the Dodge Caravan, which I had previously needed to take my late wife, Pat, to her medical appointments, for a used late model Camry. Worked on book.

September 11: Nancy was in Santa Fe for the opera, and we talked by email and telephone, discussing the current tennis tournament [U.S. Open] at which Emma Raducanu and Leyla Fernandez were playing. Worked on book.

September 15: Read Goren's book on bridge. Trying to relearn bridge bidding rules.

September 17-21: Drove to Austin to stay with Nancy Friday-Sunday. Visited with Nancy's daughter-in-law, Yami Labastida; Nancy's granddaughter, Adriana; and Adriana's boyfriend, Matt. Nancy's son, Fernando Augusto Labastida, cooked for us. Nancy and I played bridge with Nancy's friend Abby and her husband, Jim. Drove back to Dallas. Back in Dallas, I emailed Etta James singing "At Last" to Nancy.

September 24-26: Nancy drove to Dallas and stayed at La Quinta. Nancy and I visited with John and Louise Kee, then John and Jo Guittard, enjoying dinner at Lavendou Restaurant on far north Preston Road, and finally had breakfast with Mike and Ginnie Amis at La Madeline Restaurant. Nancy and I discussed my moving in with her in Austin; Nancy says she can find me a cubbyhole for my things.

September 30, Thursday: 5 a.m. I sent an email to Nancy about setting up an expense account for my share of expenses upon my moving into her house. At 6 a.m., Nancy responded via email saying she liked my email. At 8:50 a.m., as Nancy was on her way to get a COVID shot in Kyle, Texas, I called her, she answered, and I said: "Nancy, I have a question for you... (long pause). Will you marry me?" Nancy, answering without a pause, "Yes." I agreed not to make a general announcement to anyone until she had had a chance to break the news to her siblings. It was thirty-nine days after first contact on August 22.

October 1-December 10, 2021: Preparations for our marriage occurred at a rapid clip, including deciding that Nancy's Methodist pastor brother Talbot would conduct the ceremony at Nancy's house, that Bill Oliver would provide the music with his guitar, that Adriana would take wedding photos, and Yami's family catering business would provide the food; Nancy went window shopping for an engagement ring after we agreed on a budget; we requested an Austin estate attorney to prepare a prenuptial agreement to put our family members at ease; The Reserve at North Dallas gave me until November 30 to move out of my apartment; Nancy and I dined at Al Biernat in Dallas with my friends John Glancy and Carole Adams; I took boxes to storage on multiple days; watched Baylor team beat Texas 35-21 on television; moved one hundred fifty books from my apartment into stacks in the hall outside for whoever wanted them; Nancy and I picked up Nancy's ring at the jeweler; lined up Junk Haulers to clear out large stuff I couldn't give away; gave a number of musical instruments and pieces of furniture to Broderick Mosely ("Mo"), husband of Pat's devoted caregiver Mary Hayes; Nancy and I drove to get a marriage license. I had my last pre-wedding haircut by Champagne in Richardson; attended the 106th birthday celebration of Betty X Labastida (Nancy's mother) in Buda, Texas, with Nancy; I moved into Nancy's home on November 30.

December 11: Nancy and I were married at Nancy's home by Reverend Talbot Davis. Bill Oliver sang an Elvis song as we were soberly standing with Talbot after finishing the vows.

December 12-14: Nancy and I embarked on a quick honeymoon in Galveston, Texas, at the Tremont Hotel. In Galveston, we dined at Gaido's Seafood Restaurant, walked The Strand, had frozen margaritas at Murdoch's, took a ferry ride to Bolivar Island, had dinner at Willy G's, and drove back to Austin, promising we would take a longer trip later.

PART I

The Chase (The Emails)

Note: The emails below have been excerpted to shorten them and avoid repetition, but they have not been revised to comply with rules of spelling, punctuation, or grammar, and some information has been redacted or changed for privacy.

<hr/>

"ONE FOR THE MONEY": THE DAY AFTER CONTACT

Nancy Labastida

To: Charles Guittard

Monday, August 23, 2021, 9:24 a.m.

I just got off the treadmill, where I do my best thinking. You really planted a seed in my mind about writing a book, and I was recalling many sweet, sad, happy and bittersweet memories about my life as a tennis player. I've had my shower and I must get on with my day. First I need to run errands and then meet up with my tennis team for brunch/lunch. I'm not playing this summer, because I had a scare with heat exhaustion on the first hot day. Then I have friendly, competitive bridge in the afternoon. Find a good reason to visit your son and family. *Hehehe.*

Charles Guittard

To: Nancy Labastida

Monday, August 23, 2021, 9:50 a.m.

As to bridge, I used to play regularly and would enter duplicate tournaments in Waco and Dallas. I also played with high school buddies quite a bit. I took lessons from Nancy Touchstone. I also occasionally played bridge against Florence Files who played Culbertson rather than Scheinwold or Goren. You may remember the brilliant Mrs. Files who taught math at Franklin; her son Sid was my best friend in high school and still plays tennis every day in San Diego. Alas, I no longer play tennis or bridge, but I could probably get back into bridge with a little (or lot) of brushing up. I used to read Bobby Wolff's columns from time to time.

—————— •◦❈◦• ——————

Charles Guittard

To: Nancy Labastida

Monday, August 23, 2021, 4:50 p.m.

My favorite bid was always 3 no trump but I can't remember the number of high card points needed for that bid. There was something called Stayman that was cool too and various other conventions locked away somewhere in my gray matter. I persuaded my father to buy a thick book on bridge theory by Marshall Miles. He bought it but I remember him asking me, "Charles, are you really going to read this book?" and I said "sure!" And I did read some of it, but it was heavy going after a while and that was that. I preferred Goren's book which I could mostly understand.

Nancy Labastida

To: Charles Guittard

Monday, August 23, 2021, 4:55 p.m.

My phone number is [removed for privacy]. My partner was down one.

Nancy Labastida

To: Charles Guittard

Monday, August 23, 2021, 8:17 p.m.

You know a heck of a lot about bridge. I like to play for fun and socializing, but I also play competitive, but not seriously. I do have some master points, but only because I like competition. I do believe that Goren is by far the best teacher and system. I have played with people that have all kinds of fancy conventions, and it seems that they trip all over themselves.

Since our father was a professor, all of us were able to go to SMU free. My parents had eight children plus one adopted sister. Of those nine, six of us graduated from SMU [undergraduate]...The next to youngest went to Centenary on a partial tennis scholarship. The youngest went to Princeton, because by that time my parents had made a lot of money by investing in real estate (land)! The one who went to Centenary, went to SMU Law School, so he is also an SMU graduate. We grew up in the glory days of the Southwest Conference. We did not like Baylor, but not nearly as much as we disliked UT and Texas A&M!!!

Since Covid, I have been playing bridge on Bridge Base Online. There are hundreds of bridge players that have been playing on line for years and who have not played in person for 10 or 20 years. It was a real eye opener for me. Well, it's been a long day.

Charles Guittard

To: Nancy Labastida

Monday, August 23, 2021, at 10:09 p.m.

I did not expect to hear from you again today as I had convinced myself I was becoming annoying.

I played with Esther Alverson's duplicate group at the Meadows Building a couple of times. I also played a couple of times at the Raleigh Hotel in Waco with my roommate. He played under an assumed name because if we happened to place—which we did— they printed the names in the newspaper. Larry's father was a Baptist preacher and I guess didn't approve of bridge or other game of that sort. I've been a Methodist, Baptist, and Presbyterian, and the Baptists were overly strict about some things at that time.

Baylor's primary enemies in sports were Texas and A&M. Baylor would play A&M every other year at homecoming. The freshmen were required to guard the campus against the Aggies because we were convinced they would do bad things to the campus the night before homecoming. There was an incident in maybe 1937 in which the Baylor cheerleaders made fun of the Aggies, it pissed off the Aggies who tried to pull Baylor girls off a float, and Baylor students rushed to the rescue; one Baylor guy took a wooden folding chair and brained an Aggie who died the next day. Baylor and A&M didn't play each other for four years after that.

I was an SMU guy (My football heroes were Doak Walker, Kyle Rote, Johnny Champion, Dick McKissack, etc.) until I was shipped off to Waco. Dr. Aaron Sartain of SMU's business school lived across the street and they were naturally really big on Doak Walker and I was too.

Nancy Labastida

To: Charles Guittard

Tuesday, August 24, 2021, at 9:03 a.m.

No, you were not annoying. I was playing bridge, so I had to answer in short, quick sentences, which were a bit more suitable for texting. I didn't really play much bridge in Dallas. I learned when some friends asked me to fill in, when they were playing in the SMU student center. They told me basic rules that day, and I took to it right away. However, classes and boys were far more important to me then, so I rarely played. I started playing bridge again in London because I needed to make friends. I joined the American Women's Club and started playing twice a week and learned a lot. Soon, I got heavily involved with my tennis club, which was just a block away from our house. Almost all of my tennis friends also played bridge, so I played more and more often. When we retired to Austin, I immediately got involved with the tennis world here, but bridge was in the background. Now tennis is in the background, and bridge is in my main activity.

I was raised Episcopalian, but I gave up organized religion while I was at SMU. It was so freeing. The youngest of the Davis children, Talbot, is a Methodist minister in Charlotte, NC. He calls himself the white sheep of the family. He was born when I was 20 and a senior at SMU. Our family was passionate, to put it mildly, about SMU. My parents had season tickets to the football games, and we kids took turns going to the games. I saw Doak Walker and Johnny Champion play many times. My parents were good friends with the Sartains. Their son Richard was one of my brother Harvey's best friends. Where did you live during your high school days? Where do you live now?

I was reading what you wrote about yourself on Classmates. I also love true crime on television. I especially like Dateline.

Charles Guittard

To: Nancy Labastida

Tuesday, August 24, 2021, at 9:30 a.m.

I am addicted to Forensic Files, Dr. Pimple Popper (less so), and Hoarders (even less so). More later.

Nancy Labastida

To: Charles Guittard

Tuesday, August 24, 2021, at 9:41 a.m.

Back to tennis and Northwood. There were times when I was on the court with Nancy Swenson, Nancy Penson, and Nancy Sommerville. We all found that quite amusing. The Pensons came to London every year for Wimbledon. One year, they asked me if I could arrange a mixed doubles game on the grass at my club one morning before they would go to Wimbledon in the afternoon, so I did. They came out to my quaint English club, and my friend and I played mixed doubles against them. We won. Then they showered and went off to Wimbledon with their driver. You seem to know so many tennis players at Northwood. Was your family a member there?

Nancy Labastida

To: Charles Guittard

Tuesday, August 24, 2021, at 9:44 a.m.

Hehehe. I cannot watch Dr. Pimple Popper. I have watched Hoarders with morbid fascination, but I find it painful and sad. My dirty little secret is that I love Toddlers and Tiaras. There, I've confessed.

Charles Guittard

To: Nancy Labastida

Tuesday, August 24, 2021, at 1:27 p.m.

Yes, my parents were members at Northwood where my father played golf, not very well, but he didn't devote much time to it and was not extremely coordinated—he dropped typing in high school because of a lack of dexterity in his hands. My brother and I played tennis and occasionally golf. I was very mediocre at tennis and terrible at golf. Probably terrible at both but much better at tennis. Sid Files's family were members at the Dallas Athletic Country Club where Leo Laborde was the pro. That's where I saw Ham Richardson play one time. I remember hitting a few balls with Mike Amis—you probably remember Amis since he played at SMU. I remember one time he was just playing around with me, goofing off I guess, and when he served, he would throw up three balls in the air and just hit one of them which I'm sure he thought was funny and would confuse me and it did. I also felt "dissed" if not "pissed." Later on, at a time when Mike and I were both attorney-mediators and acolytes of Steve Brutsche [early leader of the mediation movement in Texas], we bonded at some level, I changed my early view of Mike, and he and I joined a team of Dallas mediators to train mediators in California. I was involved in doing a number of trainings back then; my agenda was helping attorneys settle their cases out of court, cut legal costs, and do their clients a favor, rarely a popular position with the defense bar which billed by the hour.

Jack Penson's name, Gordon Galt's, and Al Oldham's were always high up on the men's tennis ladder, probably with your dad's too. I had a pretty good forehand and serve—a hard flat serve—but a weak backhand and slow reflexes at the net. I never have been able to figure out how to do the "American twist serve" that all the pros use. Of course, I never figured out how to do a golf swing either. Most of my friends at Hillcrest were really smart guys but they were often pitiful at tennis and not much better at bridge. They went on MIT, Dartmouth, and the Ivy League, but my guess is they never got any better at tennis or bridge. Of course, they were often self-taught at bridge and didn't read books on bridge; my mother paid for me to have lessons from Nancy Touchstone, a teacher of beginning bridge players, and then I read Bobby Wolff's columns and Goren on the side.

I went to the Wimbledon facility in 1963 with a group of college kids and we took a walk through it. There were some SMU and UT girls on that trip and just a few boys so it seemed to be a pretty good deal to be one of those few guys. The bad news is that the ones I was attracted to were either engaged or had boyfriends back in the U.S. I was the baggage boy which was an easy job and we got a small discount on the costs of the trip. So tell me more about your days as a competitive tennis player.

Charles Guittard

To: Nancy Labastida

Tuesday, August 24, 2021, at 1:34 p.m.

I was about to say "Dr. Pimple Popper" is an acquired taste but that sounds a little weird so I won't. Never watched "Toddlers and

Tiaras." Sounds like something guys would change the channel on. I've watched a few "Forged in Fire" episodes and those cupcake shows but I never really got into them. "Iron Chef" and some of those are OK. "Beat Bobby Flay" is interesting. I guess "Chopped" is my favorite. Although I'm not a fan of all this zombie mania in the movie and T.V. industry, I did like The Walking Dead and its sequel. I was also addicted to Dexter but had to give it up it was so sick.

Nancy Labastida

To: Charles Guittard

Tuesday, August 24, 2021, at 4:30 p.m.

Wow, it's almost like we walked hand in hand through our childhood. I am very familiar with just about every name you casually mention in your emails. It is so interesting that you also went to Northwood as a child. My siblings and I were there every day in the summer and frequently in the winter. There were 8 of us, and usually someone (like you) would know at least one of us, but you fall between Virginia and me, and we never knew you. During the summer between my junior and senior years in high school, we moved to University Park, so I actually graduated from Highland Park, as did all my younger siblings. Only the oldest, Libby, graduated from Hillcrest. When I was very young, we lived in Highland Park, and I went to Bradfield, so I did have friends at HP. When I lived on South Versailles, it was one block from Mike Amis, who lived in the same block, but on North Versailles. He was a year or so younger and was not very nice to me. He wasn't mean; he just wasn't nice. A few years ago, Harvey and I drove up to Dallas for Leo LaBorde Sr.'s memorial, and Mike Amis was there. He was charming and friendly, and every negative thing I ever felt about him, immediately left me. He was lovely, as was his wife.

Ham Richardson played often at Northwood, and he played some of the same tournaments I played in around Texas. My father played singles every Thursday morning and Sunday afternoon (I think) with Dr. Hal Moore. Dad could make sure he had no classes on Thursday morning, and Dr. Moore was a pediatrician, and he didn't have office hours on Thursday morning. We also swam at Northwood. I can't remember if the big swim was 4th of July or Labor Day. So, you actually played my brother?

I would love to tell you all about my days as a competitive tennis player, but it would fill a book! Hahaha. It would be all about me. I would say my competitive days spanned decades and had three major sections: junior in Texas, adult in London, senior in Austin. I'll write more in another email. I've played bridge for 3 hours on line with my friends from Austin. Tonight I will play in a fun, friendly tournament, so I'm charging my IPad, and I need a little rest.

Charles Guittard

To: Nancy Labastida

Tuesday, August 24, 2021, at 5:14 p.m.

I'm on the way to pick up a pork chop waiting for me down in the kitchen, so I'm not a vegan today. My main July 4th Northwood story is the swimming competition. There were only two entrants in our category, me and Billy Hightower, Coach Hightower's son. You probably can guess what I'm about to say. The race was one lap to other end of the pool and back to the starting place. The gun sounded, we both dove in the water. Billy was a short little guy, not impressive to look at. Anyway, I made it to the other end of the pool and did the turnaround and thought I would look to see where Billy was—he was already back [at] the other end of the pool and almost ready to get out. Billy got a little trophy to go along with all of his other trophies and I learned an important lesson: don't think you can beat small guys just because they are small. I'm just lucky it wasn't a martial arts thing. Challenge little guys—unless they are

Asian—to ping pong. I was fair at ping pong, but I couldn't do anything fancy since I used a sandpaper paddle.

Whenever I get down to Austin, I hope you will give me a demo of how the online bridge thing works. I don't have a clue. I will pick up a Goren book to refresh so I will at least remember the bidding.

------ ⋅⚬⟩⟨⚬⋅ ------

Nancy Labastida

To: Charles Guittard

Tuesday, August 24, 2021, at 6:13 p.m.

I can absolutely picture Billy Hightower's little tiny body. It always bewildered me how that robust man could produce such a small son. I suppose he grew up to be normal size. Coach Hightower taught me and all of my siblings how to swim. My siblings and I almost always won our age division swimming races. I was very competitive and hated to lose.

Well, Charles, I am probably going to Dallas on September 24, so I can show you how the online bridge thing works then. First of all go to Bridge Base On Line (BBO) and have a look.

------ ⋅⚬⟩⟨⚬⋅ ------

Charles Guittard

To: Nancy Labastida

Tuesday, August 24, 2021, at 6:50 p.m.

I will look forward to that on September 24. I'm hoping to get to Austin before then—it depends on scheduling in Austin of the guy's games. Bob is going to let me know. I certainly welcome you to my teeny tiny apartment on Sept 24, whether or not we meet before then or not—816 square feet complete with kitchen, a bedroom, bath, and my office, where I am writing my book. We downsized when we moved to Dallas and found a senior community that would provide support for Pat who was diagnosed with dementia in 2013. I haven't moved out because I had only a few months left until my book would be ready for my publisher and then *hasta luego*, Senior Living! I will be studying bridge per your suggestions.

Nancy Labastida

To: Charles Guittard

Tuesday, August 24, 2021, at 7:10 p.m.

I'm getting ready to start my bridge tournament soon. I would love to see you in Austin. I'll write more later.

Nancy Labastida

To: Charles Guittard

Tuesday, Aug 24, 2021, at 9:23 p.m.

I just finished the bridge tournament, and my partner and I won. He makes daring bids, and his play is dazzling and sometimes confuses the opponents. He is way better than I am, but I'm steady and reliable. He lives in Canada, and I'll never meet him in person, but we enjoy playing together on line.

It must be so freeing to downsize, and it is very kind to your children to do so. How heroic and fine of you to care for your wife for so long. It is such a noble and admirable thing to do. Do you know where you will go when you leave senior living? How exciting that your book is so near ready to go to the publisher.

Charles Guittard

To: Nancy Labastida

Tuesday, August 24, 2021, at 9:58 p.m.

First, congratulations on winning the tournament. That's great. I feel I will be able to get back into bridge and then we'll see. I know though, I'm never going to be the guy that remembers all the cards that have been played, etc., etc. But I'll play Goren and do O.K. I was playing with my brother and my uncle and cousin Steve one time who were paired together. At the end of one hand, my uncle—an overbearing prosecutor type—took his adult son to task for mistakes doing this or that in either bidding the hand, playing it or both, and it was a pretty uncomfortable scene. During the harangue, I realized that my uncle had it all wrong and I pointed that out, to my cousin's delight.

Don't know where I'll go from Senior Living. Bob wants me to move to Austin. But for the time being, it's going to be Dallas and the future will be whatever the future will be. It does feel good not to have to worry about wrapping the water pipes when a freeze is predicted or watching out for termites, or huddling in a safe room when a hurricane or tornado is blowing in. And if I want to look at my stuff I don't have room for, I can just get in my car and drive a few blocks down the road to the storage unit, take a flashlight, and have a good old time poking around in that old stuff. I'm kidding here a little—I don't much like poking around in that stuff and wish it would all go away to wherever it should go to without me having to spend another minute down there But I have two trombones, a nice mantel clock, some pieces of art, some furniture, all my tax records, my book collection, a harp, and other things.

Nancy Labastida

To: Charles Guittard

Wednesday, August 25, 2021, at 7:40 a.m.

I often think of moving to a place where I won't have to worry about wrapping pipes or paying property tax! The property tax might drive me out of my house one day, although seniors can delay paying taxes on their houses, but the taxes will have to be paid with interest when the house changes hands. Every year, I ponder that option, but so far have not taken it up.

I look around my house with bittersweet memories and wonder what my children or siblings will want eventually. I have some art from my parents' house and a lot that my husband and I collected over the years. It's all very personal and meaningful to me, but who knows who will care in the end? For the time being, I'm staying right here and enjoying life as much as I can during Covid.

Charles Guittard

To: Nancy Labastida

Wednesday, August 25, 2021, at 8:59 a.m.

Today I head to Waco to deliver the framed illustrations [by Amanda Hope Smith, now Colborn] of scenes from my grandfather's life along with that plaque you saw on FB. I will have to find a jacket and I suppose slacks in my closet unless I want to look like I don't give a damn about convention in a situation (the dedication of the renovated Tidwell building today) that they already told me to dress up. If I have an ace in the hole, it's that I'm a senior citizen and maybe they'll cut me some slack. Whether I wear a jacket and slacks or not, I will be wearing shoes that look more or less like tennis shoes.

What to do with those things in storage will be a problem for someone someday. I have a clock that was in my great grandfather's house in New Bedford, Ohio and that was later in my grandfather's and then father's houses in Waco and Dallas respectively. I remember my mother trying to get me to come and clear my things from my school days out of their garage attic on Desco and it was like pulling teeth.

I went to a birthday party for my sister Mary (71 years) last night at their house attended my brother John and myself and Hank and Mary. The evening started off in a weird way as their tiny schnauzer Maverick jumped me when I came in the front door and started humping the back of my leg! You may remember Rodney Dangerfield's line about not getting any sex—the only sex he's had lately is when a pickpocket stole his wallet. I must close, eat the usual oatmeal, gas up the car, and get on I-35.

Nancy Labastida

To: Charles Guittard

Wednesday, August 25, 2021, at 9:03 a.m.

Charles, I loved your fun and humorous email!!! I go to a personal trainer for one hour a week! Hahaha That doesn't do too much good, but she helps me with balance and agility. I'm going today, just before the birthday party. I would love to have been at that birthday party last night. Drive carefully; stay safe.

Nancy Labastida

To: Charles Guittard

Wednesday, August 25, 2021, at 1:23 p.m.

Well, since you asked about my junior tennis and said you were all ears, I have been thinking about it. I'll try to be brief. I started playing in tournaments maybe at age 9 or 10. I almost never won a match. I often got a bye and a default and ended up in the finals against my arch rival, Martha Walker from Garland. She had a wicked slice and a very unorthodox game and drove me crazy.

My father was always there to watch my matches, and he never showed emotion, which is wonderful for a tennis parent. I was mostly afraid of my father and uncomfortable with him, but at tennis matches, he was just what I needed. I don't think I realized it at the time. After I would lose yet another match, my father would always say, "Chalk it up to experience." At the same time, I was on a junior swimming team at the Highland Park swimming pool. We would go there in the morning and Northwood in the afternoon. We swam laps and took swimming very seriously. I always won my swimming events.

We moved away from Highland Park and out to Churchill Way, which was in the country then. One summer, I pretty much gave up swimming and decided to concentrate on tennis, and I also decided I'd had enough experience in losing! So that summer, I won my first tournament and beat Walker. I was 12, and from then on, I almost never lost. I went to Texas Sectionals when I was 14 to play in the 15 and under category and won. I beat Nancy Richey in the finals. It was lucky I'd never heard of her. Nancy went on to beat me in the finals of Texas Sectionals when I was 15 and one more time before she stopped playing piddly little matches in Texas!!! So the next year, when I was 16, I had to play in the 18 and under division, and I didn't expect to win much, but to my enormous surprise, I won Texas Sectionals again and won all that summer. The next summer, I was 17 and had just graduated from Highland Park. It was 1958. Sectionals are in June at the beginning of the season. Lightning struck again, and I won the 18 and under group for my third Sectionals win.

After Sectionals, I knew every girl in Texas was gunning for me. Every girl in Texas beat me all summer long. Mercifully, I started SMU in the fall and almost never picked up a racket again until I moved to London in 1977, even though I still had one more year of eligibility. I did not miss tennis one bit during that long break. I did go to Nationals in Chicago twice to play girls 15 and under, but I did not do well. Tennis was a big deal to me, but I don't think I was ever going to give it what it takes to go beyond where I was. Also, I was boy crazy and my social life a big deal to me.

Oddly, I never did well in playing for my high school to go to State. I didn't really understand the significance of State. All my emphasis was on the summer tournaments. I only went to State one time, my senior year at Highland Park. I got upset by some girl that I beat a month later at Sectionals. I blame it on the weather in Austin! It rained for at least 2 days, so when we finally started, I was just off my game. Also, I didn't like that girl who beat me, and it all got in my head.

This was not brief! The cities where I played most of my junior tournaments were Dallas, San Antonio, Wichita Falls, Shreveport, Houston, Beaumont (once) Greenville, Commerce, Tyler, Waco, and Ft. Worth. In those days, when we would drive into Greenville, there was a banner hanging across the main street that said, "Welcome to Greenville with the whitest people and the blackest earth." I hated that so much, but I will never forget it. I'd better stop, or we will have nothing to talk about, if and when we do get together in person!!!

Nancy Labastida

To: Charles Guittard

Wednesday, August 25, 2021, at 1:36 p.m.

Now that I think about it, I'm pretty sure that the Greenville sign more likely read like this: "Welcome to Greenville. The blackest land and the whitest people."

Charles Guittard

To: Nancy Labastida

Wednesday, August 25, 2021, at 7:00 p.m.

I've heard the saying about Greenville but can't remember exactly which way it goes. Either way, it's a problem for me too and a remnant of the South's racist past and, to some extent, present. I, by the way am a Democrat too, not a life-long one like my grandfather or like you, but a newly minted and passionate one. My father was a conservative Democrat as long as the Democrat candidates for judgeships won and a moderate Republican after one had to be a Republican to hold on to one's elective office. Father was a district judge for ten or more years and associate justice and then chief justice of the Dallas Court of Appeals. He and your dad would have known each other although traveling in different legal circles. They wouldn't have played tennis at Northwood either because Father's game was weak (I could beat him soundly); besides, he worked five days a week and a half a day or more on Saturdays, and I'm sure on Sundays when preparing for a trial as a trial attorney.

BTW there is a chapter in the book I totally made up about book-selling in Greenville. I didn't get into the race thing though. I get into the race thing in another chapter I call Waco and the KKK. Patricia Bernstein was one or two years behind me at Hillcrest and wrote a well-researched book called *The First Waco Horror.* I used some of the stuff in her book for the KKK chapter. Her book is a cautionary non-fiction chronicle of how white supremacy grows and mutates, etc., etc., but this is getting way too heavy for a light email.

Charles Guittard

To: Nancy Labastida

Wednesday, August 25, 2021, at 7:54 p.m.

I really enjoyed this piece [Nancy's tennis career]. Very much. That does *not* mean that you need to feel guilty if you are not interested in writing a chapter 2. I do suspect it could be woven into a much larger tapestry with multiple themes, metaphors, turning points, and perhaps even paradoxes. As one example only, the father-daughter thing is obviously interesting and one would want to see how it went when you were not on the tennis court. I know I'm not being very clear. But I think there's a story there. Somehow, the line from the "Music Man" comes to mind: "Kid, I always think there's a band somewhere." My belief is that nearly anyone's life can be told interestingly if there is enough material—it would seem you have a ton of material and another possible plus—a lot of siblings with information. You may not be interested in doing any more writing, but I think you could shape a book in any way that you wanted.

Nancy Labastida

To: Charles Guittard

Wednesday, August 25, 2021, at 9:12 p.m.

I am just thrilled to hear that you are a newly minted, passionate Democrat. It really is a wonderful thing to know someone like you. It can't be easy to change, so it is very, very admirable. I feel sure that our fathers knew each other. My father started out practicing law, but he found out pretty quickly that the practice of law didn't suit him; he felt like he had to compromise his beliefs. He joined the faculty at SMU Law School and found his niche. He often joined with like-minded students on their cases after they graduated. He had quite a few lawyer friends with whom he was involved in cases. Our parents seem very similar, although my father was an extrovert without really good social skills!!!

Yes, my late husband Fernando was a comparative law student. His year at SMU meant the world to him, although he was disappointed that his scholarship didn't send him to his first choice—Columbia. He loved being invited to anything by host families. The year that he was at SMU was the year that my father took a sabbatical, starting in January, so he was not as involved with the foreign students as he usually was. My parents and my 6 younger siblings went to Spain that January and came back in the summer. I met Fernando is April, shortly before he graduated. I wrote to my parents about him, and when they came back, we were already engaged. I love and miss you. *Nancy*

Charles Guittard

To: Nancy Labastida

Wednesday, August 25, 2021, at 10:26 p.m.

My trip to Waco today was exhausting and I'm lucky a policeman didn't catch me zooming down there to meet my illustrator. I did get to see President Livingstone [Baylor] cut the ribbon—she was outside on the front steps, I was inside looking through her legs, when she used some giant scissors to cut the ribbon. I never speed but on occasion I do. I started late and there were a lot of traffic snarls on I-35.

Nancy Labastida

To: Charles Guittard

Thursday, August 26, 2021, at 6:13 a.m.

Hi again, Charles. I am interested in writing chapter 2, and I really skimmed over chapter 1. A teacher at Hillcrest once told the class that we should start right then to write down about our lives because we could all write a good autobiography. I have regretted many times not having followed her advice. I did keep a diary, but I'm afraid that and many other things I treasured were lost when my parents moved to Austin. My mother gave away most of the trophies I won to underprivileged children who played in little tennis tournaments she organized. I saved the ones I cherished the most. I would like to write chapter 2, that takes place in London…

Charles Guittard

To: Nancy Labastida

Thursday, August 26, 2021, at 7:52 a.m.

I wish I had had your high school teacher if only to hear the advice about keeping a diary. One great thing about a diary is that one is in control of the entries and stuff that is too painful to record need not be included. The good news about not keeping a diary is that many of our brains do retain a lot of information that can be called up even without submitting to hypnosis. Bob wants to interview me about my life before I'm NCM and I made an outline of topics to hit. There were a lot of them. Now where the H did I put that list?

BTW, another thing we are potentially talking about is legacy. To me, that doesn't just mean the things, the cash and real property, mutual funds, the photos, the jewelry, the watch and the old shoes and all those things in the bank deposit box, but something much more important—who their father, mother was as a person, and something of the challenges they had to face, their personality, what made them unique. One of my other beliefs is that our children and grandchildren whose sense of self and purpose is evolving can be strengthened in some way by feeling they connect with their grandfather, even if they never knew them. That is the way I feel about my grandfather Frank Guittard. I never really knew him in life, but have gained knowledge of him through correspondence, diaries, papers he wrote in college or grad school, and interviews with my father.

The bottom line is that if we don't leave at least some breadcrumbs for them (our children and grandchildren), they will never ever find their way back to who we really were. Now I wish I hadn't thrown away the only debate trophy my partner [and I] won in high school—the Brownwood Tournament at Howard Payne University in which Jerry G– and I defeated 4-1 the team from Houston Kinkaid H.S. Nor will they ever know about the moot court teams and the negotiation teams I co-coached to first place in a number of tournaments.

I will send you another email much later on after I get my haircut–I still have a lot of hair! And all of my teeth. My grandfather dyed his hair in his last 20 years and I'm tempted to let my barber put a slight color in my hair. Hmm, that's a hard decision, since it would only make a slight difference in the color.

Nancy Labastida

To: Charles Guittard

Thursday, August 26, 2021, at 8:20 a.m.

Just a brief note before I go visit my mother. I have in person bridge this afternoon, as I do every Thursday. I love everything you have written. There is so much to absorb, that I will reread again later. Two things about our similarities that stand out. My father and your grandfather had very similar beginnings to their academic lives and their careers, and my father and mother were from Ohio. My father's passion at SMU was the moot court team.

By the way, I have no business recommending anything, but if I did, I would recommend not coloring your hair. From my perspective, a man with colored hair loses all sex appeal. There, I've said it. I have been very lucky with my hair, and I do not color it. It saves so much time and money. On the other hand, how wonderful that you have a lot of hair and your own teeth! I also have my teeth, thank goodness.

Charles Guittard

To: Nancy Labastida

Thursday, August 26, 2021, at 9:23 a.m.

That's funny. I have a lot of hair and teeth but I'm not sure the final result is that sexy anymore if it ever was.

———————————

Charles Guittard

To: Nancy Labastida

Thursday, August 26, 2021, at 11:16 a.m.

I would like to come to Austin and visit. I know you said you are generally available except for your planned trip to Santa Fe. I had in mind coming say in middle afternoon, visiting, and going somewhere to eat (your choice) that is convenient and not too noisy and then continuing our conversation the following morning if we haven't already talked ourselves out and become tired of each other, after which I will drive back to Dallas. I may or may not be in my van (wheelchair accessible) I bought so I could take dear Pat out to restaurants and then during Covid through drive-throughs. I'm thinking a wheelchair-accessible van is not the right vibe I want to send out and so may go to a Toyota of some kind. So I want to find out whether any of these days would work for you. My complication is boarding Maggie so the earlier you let me know the better it would be so I can make a reservation at Ruffitt: August 31-Sept 8; Sept 13-19. I don't know whether I will be overnighting at Bob and Candace's with their crew or not. Their planning has to take into consideration all five of their schedules.

Nancy Labastida

To: Charles Guittard

Thursday, August 26, 2021, at 11:44 a.m.

Wow, Charles! I could hardly wait to get home to tell you that my brother Harvey remembers you!! August 31-September 8, would work, but surely you mean a day or two during that time. Sept. 3-5 work the best. Also Sept, 17-19 works. I can always cancel a bridge game, or play so you can see how it works. Actually, I can cancel anything when something more important happens, like a visitor from out of town. Thursdays are difficult because I play in person and hate to miss it, and sometimes it's tough to find a sub. My address is [removed for privacy]. My telephone number is [removed for privacy].

Charles Guittard

To: Nancy Labastida

Thursday, August 26, 2021, at 2:21 p.m.

Harvey probably remembers me as one of those faceless guys he pulverized one summer afternoon and never had the chance to do it again. Who knows? Maybe even Billy Hightower remembers me too and in the same way. I will see if I can get Maggie boarded for the first set of days (Sept 3-5) and if not for the second set (Sept 17-19). As a possible alternative, what does Sept 6-8 (Mon-Wed) look like? I just mention those days because it may be a little easier to board Maggie on those days. I had my haircut and I decided against hair color. BTW, easy for you to say I shouldn't color my hair considering that you have retained your natural color. BTW2: I told my barber of our conversation and she laughed and said women always want the guy to look older.

BTW3, I stopped off at a Half-Price Books and picked up both Agassi's and Goren's books. I bought the new improved Goren's complete book on bridge, 700 pages—like I'm going to have time to do anything more than scan the table of contents before getting to Austin. The length is intimidating; even the life-long writing project of your long-winded online correspondent is barely 500 pages!

Charles Guittard

To: Nancy Labastida

Thursday, August 26, 2021, at 3:47 p.m.

The moon, stars, and venus must be aligned and I was able to get Maggie boarded for your preferred dates. I drop her off early on Friday the 3rd and head to Austin putting me in Austin sometime in the afternoon. I'm assuming that since I may be staying at a motel in your neighborhood, I'll stop off there first, check-in, and then I'll be over. I'll let you know when I've made it to wherever I'm staying.

Now to do a little cooking for Maggie—rice and chicken—since she's off the usual canned stuff and also the dry stuff.

Nancy Labastida

To: Charles Guittard

Thursday, August 26, 2021, at 4:23 p.m.

I can't believe it! That is just a week away. I will be having the bridge girls at my house the day before, so I will have tidying up to do!!! I'll be thinking of a nice quiet place for us to go, or I can cook dinner here. I usually cook salmon. My favorite restaurant is Z Tejas

Grill. What kind of food do you like? Do you like wine? If so, what kind? We can watch a bit of the US Open, too. I'm getting excited!! I love that you said the moon, stars and venus must be aligned. What kind of a dog is Maggie?

Nancy Labastida

To: Charles Guittard

Thursday, August 26, 2021, at 4:24 p.m.

Actually, Harvey remembers you as a tall boy. He said the name is very familiar.

Nancy Labastida

To: Charles Guittard

Thursday, August 26, 2021, at 4:27 p.m.

Charles, I'm glad you did not color your hair. I have mostly retained my original color, but I have a lot of gray, and I love it. I don't mind it one bit. I should have gray at my age, but I have been very lucky.

Charles Guittard

To: Nancy Labastida

Thursday, August 26, 2021, at 6:29 p.m.

Don't worry about tidying up. If your house is too tidy, then when you are in Dallas that will be a lot of pressure on me to tidy up my place, which is cluttered even after I tidy up. Leave some laundry out and we can fold it together. Maggie is 25 percent Chow-Chow, 25 percent St. Bernard, and 50 percent unknown parentage. I take her with me when we go on our nightly walks, primarily because that is the only exercise she gets during the day and because I have the idea that just seeing her might ward off a highwayman crouching in the bushes on my walk.

I like lots of different cuisines. I'm not into steak or hamburgers anymore—I love them but they are not on my list. I haven't had a glass of red wine in probably 7-10 years, but I will make an exception if we are eating at your place. And I don't do beer anymore either. Gosh this is making me sound very old-maidish or old mannish. I am partial to salmon, swordfish, almost any kind of fish other than shell-fish. As to restaurants, I am pretty catholic but excepting sushi and Indian food, both of which I like but avoid. I'll let it go at that. I don't do fried foods, come to think of it—bye bye fried chicken.

Would love to watch the U.S. open with you and have color commentary a few feet away. I'm already into the Agassi book and feeling sorry for the guy. I opened the Goren book, and said "O my God" as I looked at the TOC.

Charles Guittard

To: Nancy Labastida

Thursday, August 26, 2021, at 6:36 p.m.

Well, now Harvey's story has a little more credibility but only slightly more. I was taller than he was, possibly because I was older or perhaps just destined to be taller. I finally hit six feet and 3/4 inch before I started shrinking a little. My father was 5'8" or 5'9". I was somewhat miffed when the yardstick indicated I had lost 3/4 inch.

Nancy Labastida

To: Charles Guittard

Thursday, August 26, 2021, at 7:05 p.m.

I think Harvey is 5'11'. He had a late growth spurt. My 4 brothers were way taller than our father, and the 4 girls were way taller than our mother. The oldest, Libby, was the shortest of the girls, but she was still taller than Mom.

My visit with Mom was very sad today. She did recognize me and say "hi." She was glad to see me, but she mostly just slept. She was all bundled up and was still cold. It broke my heart, and, frankly, I think it is time for her to slip away. Mustn't be morbid; Mom has had a wonderful life.

Nancy Labastida

To: Charles Guittard

Thursday, August 26, 2021, at 7:12 p.m.

I will have to put away the bridge table and chairs, at least! Haha. Fold laundry? No. Okay, so I see that Maggie is a big dog. I was picturing a small dog. I'm sure I would like her. I like other people's dogs, but I have never had one. Well, I had one briefly, when we lived on Churchill Way, but that was a long time ago.

Well, then, it seems to me that the best idea is for me to prepare dinner on Friday night. It will be salmon and something to go with it. We'll have some wine, and we can watch the U.S. Open and look at yearbooks from Hillcrest. Unfortunately, I only have 1955 and 1956. I don't know what happened to 1957, and I have 1958 from Highland Park. I have to go now and get ready for my bridge tournament.

Nancy Labastida

To: Charles Guittard

Thursday, August 26, 2021, at 7:14 p.m.

Charles, thanks for the pictures. There is a strong family resemblance between you and your son and your darling little granddaughter.

Charles Guittard

To: Nancy Labastida

Thursday, Aug 26, 2021, at 7:27 p.m.

I may have the annuals for my years since I started in the 8th grade and graduated in 1960 so that's 56, 57, 58, 59 and 60. I'll see what I can dig up in my storage unit. I went to Highland Park Jr. In the 7th grade before my parents built the house on Desco; we moved in [and] had our first Christmas in the new house in 1955. We were still on Purdue when the house was being built. I'll bring along the originals of the 15 illustrations of scenes from my work in progress and talk you through them.

Nancy Labastida

To: Charles Guittard

Thursday, August 26, 2021, at 9:22 p.m.

Charles, it will be fun to look at the annuals, if you can find them. I went to Bradfield for grade school. I look forward to seeing the illustrations. I doubt that we will have a lull in the conversation.

Charles Guittard

To: Nancy Labastida

Thursday, August 26, 2021, at 10:01 p.m.

Historically I have tended to have a fear of running out of things to say and would make notes of topics on a little pad and put the notes in my back pocket with the idea that I would whip them out at stoplights and refresh myself. The good news is, as strange as that sounds, as it turned out, I can't remember one instance where I wanted to look back at my notes after arriving to meet a girl. They were a complete waste of time except they reduced my butterflies and that is always a good thing. I won't be making notes for our meeting as there is already so much packed in my brain from our emails, the fact that I'm a lot older than I used to be, but perhaps most importantly, I expect to be very at ease around you. Easy for me to say of course before I arrive at your front door!

Nancy Labastida

To: Charles Guittard

Friday, August 27, 2021, at 12:23 p.m.

I was just talking to my sister. She is very into astrology and signs and is always telling me when my moon in is Venus or when Mercury is in retrograde and other things that go right by me. It is very admirable that your mother resembled Nancy Reagan, especially in her unabashed adoration of your dad. Also the beauty resemblance. Nancy Reagan was beautiful and stylish. You probably know that her maiden name was Nancy Davis. I knew since I was a little kid, because we hero worshiped Hollywood actors, and I was happy that I shared my name with one, even though she was a minor actress. Needless to say, I did not admire Ronald Reagan in any way.

My birthday is May 28. Now I will read the horoscope for Scorpios every day! My close friend, tennis and bridge partner, Belva, shares your birthday. By the way, I'm thinking about dessert on next Friday. I'm thinking about a peach or apple or cherry crumble.

Charles Guittard

To: Nancy Labastida

Friday, August 27, 2021, at 2:12 p.m.

All of the dessert choices sound super. But a small slice for me, or maybe two small slices. I'm going to research the wine thing too since I may be too cautious here. The issue for me where wine is concerned is also about peeing too, to be honest, and that's not really a health thing, just comfort.

I had forgotten that Nancy Reagan's name pre-RR was Nancy Davis. I'm sure you've enjoyed that over the years. I admit I did like RR as a person, he had a sharp sense of humor, and also the other RR (Roy Rogers) and I liked Trigger, Dale, and Nellie Belle, Bullet, and everybody on their t.v. show, but not the GOP and what has become apparent about the GOP—racism, xenophobia, and lying. Al Franken wrote a book that seemed to hit the nail on the head. The SNL routine on Reagan as president is one of my favorites and is on Youtube. The same comic does the Reagan routine and also a Clinton routine which is also hilarious. My change of party affiliation actually wasn't too difficult since my feelings have eroded over a period of time—call it growing up or maturing—and then DJT ran for election and I thought "That's it!"—and I was out of there, my sister and her husband too. My cousins in New York have been Democrats forever. When Steve, who is a lawyer, interviewed with a firm for a job he reportedly asked them whether they discriminated against blacks. I will admit there was something not quite right about RR's [Reagan's] relationships with his children, I can't put my finger on it exactly.

Maggie is pretty old. I set up an appointment today for 3:30. I hope she is OK. I've got to clean the barf off the rug. She just had her annual and everything looked good. I am nervous that Maggie's issues may wreck our plan for me to come to Austin next week, but hopefully they will not and I am just being an overly nervous Nellie.

Nancy Labastida

To: Charles Guittard

Friday, August 27, 2021, at 3:12 p.m.

Oh, Charles, almost everybody liked RR. I understand that, too. My very smart brother, Talbot, who went to Princeton, loved him. He said Reagan made him feel good. Oh dear… I'm so proud of you for realizing about the GOP. Maybe, I don't have a right to "be proud of you," but that's how I feel. I admire you for realizing the truth about the Republican party. It's wonderful about your sister and her husband, too. My brother, Clayton, was elected judge in Lake Charles, LA. He ran as a Republican and was elected the first year that Obama won. Since Trump, he has become so anti everything about Trump and the Republicans. He seems as upset as we Davis Democrats.

Well, I can still show you how the bridge website works, and you can do your profile when you get back home.

Charles, of course, Maggie's comfort and health come first. It's good to be a Nervous Nellie and to be cautious. Good luck at the vet. Keep me informed.

Charles Guittard

To: Nancy Labastida

Friday, August 27, 2021, at 5:45 p.m.

Thanks, Nancy, for supporting me today. I had already cried on the way home so didn't break down during our TC. Maggie is a very sweet dog and has never caused me a moment of grief. Worry yes, grief no. We'll see what the vet says but I am almost ready to roll and just putting my show and tell together–it's not a long show so don't worry. Have you ever seen a movie called *Al Franken Saves his Family*? That's his best stuff, I think. Oh, I hope you won't be taken aback if I give you a hug when I see you.

———— ·•◦✕◦•· ————

Nancy Labastida

To: Charles Guittard

Friday, Aug 27, 2021, at 5:55 p.m.

Charles, now you are bringing tears to my eyes. I think we will have a nice long hug when we see each other. How incredibly tender that you were crying on the way home, driving without Maggie. I think we have both cried a lot over the past years. I definitely feel that tears are healing and comforting.

———— ·•◦✕◦•· ————

Charles Guittard

To: Nancy Labastida

Friday, Aug 27, 2021, at 6:09 p.m.

Good picture of both of you. Belva looks familiar. Ask her if she was born in Austin and what the name of the hospital was. I think I was born at Seton. Is there still a hospital in Austin called Seton? Maybe we were both in the first batch of the November babies. My Kee grandfather who had a large obstetrical practice (he said he delivered 10,000 children into this world), saw me crying and ordered, so his story goes, the nuns to mix up Karo syrup with something, I forget all the details of his story and he always liked to embellish them.

I'm continuing to read *Open*. It's hard to believe that Andre could be the sane mature responsible adult he is today with that creepy weird brute of a father. Steffi has to be an important part of the story. *Affectionately, Charles*

Nancy Labastida

To: Charles Guittard

Friday, August 27, 2021, at 6:32 p.m.

I just talked to Belva. Belva was actually born in Houston on Nov. 1, 1944. Your Kee grandfather sounds like another book worthy family member. I used to give my babies water with Karo syrup, when they were fussy.

About Andre Agassi, he may have had a hard driving father, but there was also something in him that made him work hard and win. Champions have that something extra that cannot be taught. Maybe it can be inspired, but it comes from within, in my humble opinion. Love, *Nancy*

Charles Guittard

To: Jim Guittard, Bob Guittard, Steve Moffatt

Friday, August 27, 2021, at 9:21 p.m.

Letting the three of you know that I've met online a nice woman that I like very much. We have been emailing multiple times a day for almost a week. Her father was an SMU Law professor I took a course from and her late husband of 50+ years received a degree in comparative law from SMU. She was a champion tennis player and swimmer in high school. She grew up playing tennis at Northwood

Country Club. She went to Hillcrest High school and then transferred to Highland Park where she graduated. She and her late husband lived in Manhattan and London for many years. Currently, she lives in Austin near her mother who is 102 [actually 105]. She is also a bridge player, playing both in-person and online. She has either eight or nine brothers and sisters; she is currently the oldest of the surviving children. Although she is slightly older than me, she is in as good or better health. She has two or three children and I don't know yet how many grandchildren. She is completely secure financially and independent and has her own house in Austin. Her name is Nancy and is a really lovely person. She is very youthful in her outlook on life and fun to communicate with.

My relationship with Nancy is very early and we still have a lot to learn about each other. We are both taking our time. I'm not announcing this to the world yet so please keep it under your hat. I have not met her in person, have had only one telephone conversation with her, but almost 90 emails, commenced initially by me. That is all for now.

Charles Guittard

To: Nancy Labastida

Friday, August 27, 2021, at 9:37 p.m.

Yes, I miss Maggie. I could not take her out on my usual walk around T. Boone Pickens Hospice. I just finished and sent a confidential email to my three sons saying I have met a lovely woman named Nancy whom I like very much who went to Hillcrest and Highland Park and was quite a tennis player. That we are taking time to get to know each other. Love, *Charles*

Nancy Labastida

To: Charles Guittard

Friday, August 27, 2021, at 9:56 p.m.

Oh, Charles, I am a little speechless about the letter that you sent to your sons. I hope they are supportive. I imagine that they would be happy for you to have found a new friend who is making you happy. I have told my two sisters and my brother, Harvey, about you, and they are very supportive. In fact, Virginia would like to know the exact time of your birth, because she wants to do your chart. I already told her your birthday, knowing she loves to know people's signs. She says that from what she can see so far, you and I are very compatible. I am presuming that you were born in 1942.

If you must know (hahaha), I was born in 1941. I was young for my grade, because I started first grade at Bradfield in a midterm class in January. I don't know why my mother put me in school so young. Anyway, when we moved out to Churchill Way, we went to Addison grade school, and there were no midterm classes there. In fact 6th, 7th and 8th grades were all in one room. It was very much a country school. Since I was pretty smart, they put me up a half a grade. Libby was also a midterm student, but she had been sick or something, so they put her back a half a grade, so Libby and I were 2 1/2 years difference in age, but one year apart in school. Libby and I were very, very close and did everything together anyway. I started Addison in the 6th grade and finished after the 8th grade, so I entered Hillcrest as a freshman. So, my point is that even though I graduated in the class of '58 [Highland Park], I should have graduated in the class of '59. I graduated from HP on my 17th birthday, and from SMU on my 21st birthday.

I haven't told my son and daughter about you yet, but it would never be a secret; I'm very open. It's all happened so fast. We can talk about our offspring when we are together. I'll be curious to know what your sons answer.

Charles Guittard

To: Nancy Labastida

Friday, August 27, 2021, at 10:43 p.m.

I already had told Jim and Bob (and thereby their wives) the gist of the email by telephone and they are supportive for exactly the reason you give. I hadn't told Steve yet (Pat's son) but he and I have a great relationship and I have no doubts about him. Actually, I don't have any doubts about my siblings or cousins either or their spouses. My only doubt is Pat's last caregiver Mary Hayes who is from New Orleans (Pat was from Louisiana, New Orleans, Hammond, and Golden Meadow) and very close to Pat through the last two years of her life including 18 months in hospice. Before helping Pat, Mary had sworn she would never take another patient who was in hospice, as it just took too much out of her. However, she and Pat became very close and it was not hard to persuade her stick with us after Pat went into hospice. When after Pat passed I raised the general subject of me going out into the world again and meeting women, Mary, who is a very spiritual person, very smart, and knows how to use a gun and a can of mace and manages a Family Dollar Store in Mesquite, went a little kookoo and said Pat would come down out of heaven and swat me. That just makes me laugh but she was serious and I really love Mary Hayes. She'll come around in time. She's a really great person, spoke at Pat's memorial service at Sparkman Hillcrest at my invitation, and Pat and I were very lucky she was assigned to us.

Nancy Labastida

To: Charles Guittard

Saturday, August 28, 2021, at 6:15 a.m.

I woke up to this most interesting and touching email. I think I love Mary Hayes! You and Pat were indeed so lucky she was assigned to you. Actually, I think people make their own luck. Mary was devoted to you and Pat because of how you treated her and how you are as people - kind and caring and all the things that I have left to learn.

My morning routine is to make my coffee and then come to the computer to check email and the bank and Facebook and then go back to the kitchen to prepare my breakfast. I'll write more after breakfast and the morning news.

Nancy Labastida

To: Charles Guittard

Saturday, August 28, 2021, at 7:22 a.m.

I usually read the newspaper, when I finish breakfast, but it hasn't come yet. I am bereft! I especially like the Saturday Austin American-Statesman, as it has The New York Times big weekend crossword puzzle, which I love. Sometimes it takes me all weekend to finish and sometimes I can finish it on Saturday, and sometimes I have to get it out of my sight, because I just can't crack [it]. It is usually my weekend companion. On Saturdays at 10:30 I play duplicate on line with Belva. The game is with the American Contract Bridge League (ACBL), and we accumulate master points, very slowly. We do it again on Sunday at 1:15.

I'm so glad that your sons understand your desire to have a new friend in your life. My children will be the same for me. They don't worry about me at all and think of me as being independent. We are very respectful of each other. If I did something they wouldn't like, though, they would not hesitate to get involved!!! My sisters would also be upset and would have plenty to say, if they thought I was doing anything risky. Charlotte has just recently moved to Houston to be near her oldest son and his wife and her grandchildren. I have already visited her in Houston.

Charles Guittard

To: Nancy Labastida

Saturday, August 28, 2021, at 9:19 a.m.

I think I have counted this correctly but tell me if I got it wrong—today we will finish our first week of knowing each other, 7 days, that's all. With 1 telephone conversation and maybe 100 emails, probably more than that, and no "in-persons. And here we are, embarked on a journey of exploration with a special new friend. Speaking of journeys, it came to me last night we might in the very near future plan a trip together somewhere. We can compare bucket lists and see if we have any matches. If there are no matches, then we can flip to see who gets to pick the trip. Or we can hire a mediator to help us negotiate a solution. I have an advantage over you there since I know all the best mediators all over Texas including in Austin. I do think it is not too soon to think about a trip together. Damn the Covid, but maybe we can work around it. And there are destinations in and around Dallas and Austin if we are not ready to get on an airplane. Wouldn't that make a great headline—"Two love-struck seniors, stricken by Covid Saturday in Saskatchewan." Or make that last word "Shanghai." I've never been to either and they would not be on my bucket list.

Charles Guittard

To: Nancy Labastida

Saturday, August 28, 2021, at 9:35 a.m.

At one point, including while studying for the bar exam, I was thinking about the fact that I really didn't want to practice law, I wanted to be a humorist writing short funny Benchley or Buchwald-like pieces. My book collection is a humor book collection which I keep in storage. But then the Draft entered my life in the mid-late 1960s and I signed up on Commerce Street to get ahead of the tank before it rolled over me. I've published a few things in *The Dallas Bar Headnotes* and in an English periodical, all satirical and making fun of established legal institutions. Some of it was not half-bad.

Nancy Labastida

To: Charles Guittard

Saturday, August 28, 2021, at 9:47 a.m.

Your humorous side is really coming out now, Charles. We probably won't need a mediator. I'm not stubborn, and I easily give in!! I love your headline about two love-struck seniors. I got married so young, but as I got older, I thought it if I were ever single again, I would love to have a relationship that included trips and dinners and dates. So, yes, a trip together any place would be on my bucket list. There are some lovely places in the Hill Country. We can eliminate Europe because of Covid.

Nancy Labastida

To: Charles Guittard

Saturday, August 28, 2021, at 9:53 a.m.

The more we communicate, the more I can see what a great writer you are. I hung on every word that Art Buchwald ever wrote. I have also seen and heard him on television. I loved him and was very lonely when he died. The Draft prompted many men to stay in school or get married or father a child. I remember those days well. Harvey was the one in my family who had to face the Draft. Another thing I used to think about that if I were ever to be single again is that I wanted a man who could make me laugh and who would think that I'm funny. *N xoxo*

Charles Guittard

To: Nancy Labastida

Saturday, August 28, 2021, at 10:02 a.m.

You are obviously more orderly than I am. I go straight to email to see what has come in and then I immediately start responding. All the while I'm hungry and listening to my stomach growling. And/or Maggie growling wanting to be taken out. I don't do crossword puzzles: first, because they are too hard and I don't want to feel like a failure just as I am starting my day; second, because I see all these old people at my facility diligently working on their puzzles to keep their brains functioning while wondering whether they need to buy a new cane or walker or one of those little scooters; and third, because I get a lot of stimulation working on my writing project and in the last week writing messages to dear Nancy.

I don't have a lot planned today. I am thinking about looking for a car to replace the van I can drive to Austin. We'll see whether that happens. I need to do my tax return for 2020. I may go to that new Marvel movie entitled something like Shang Kai, Master of Kung Fu. You may think I'm joking but I'm not. I used to read that comic, it was well scripted, well-drawn, and several cuts above the usual stuff. I used to collect comics as I kid but my parents, probably my mother, threw them away—*Can you hear me, Mother, you made a mistake; those would have been very valuable?!!* I started collecting again in the 1970s but gave them away to Steve who may have sold them on Ebay.

Nancy Labastida

To: Charles Guittard

Saturday, August 28, 2021, at 10:14 a.m.

Charles, you have me laughing out loud now. Your subject line— "Dear old pal of seven days!" Hahahaha. I've been working crossword puzzles since I was in college. I inspired my mother to start doing them, and she did them as long as she could. We both love words and writing. We played Scrabble several times a week for years.

I finally got my paper, but I won't be able to tackle the crossword until after the bridge tournament. I finally got my 2020 taxes filed. Enjoy the movie, if you go. I'm glad you are going before you come to Austin, because we might have had to hire a mediator to decide which movie we would want to see together. My mother threw away a lot of sentimental things that were left behind, but nothing as valuable and as special as a comic book collection. I had a lot of Archie comic books.

Charles Guittard

To: Nancy Labastida

Saturday, August 28, 2021, at 10:41 a.m.

Your son is really right of course. He has a lot of common sense, like you. He is your son and he loves his mom. But "Jeezus!" I'm almost 79, you are 80, if my math is correct and it may not be. And neither one of us is going to do anything foolish and we have a lot of people potentially looking on and giving us feedback. We are both independent financially and have sufficient assets to carry us comfortably through our old ages without depleting our kiddoes' inheritances or diminishing our charitable legacies. I don't think that saying "There's no fool like an old fool" applies to either of us. And both of our lives—especially mine and I suspect yours to some extent—have been on hold as we held our loved ones' hands through their terminal illnesses. Pat's lasted at least seven years, with hospice being only the last 18 months.

The main question is how well we get along with each other when we get to hang around each other in person and whether there is some annoying trait that will surface that spoils the soup. I don't expect that to happen. I only expect my affection for you to grow as I get a better sense of who you are and have been. Well, it's time for me to grab the usual oatmeal and turkey sausage. I'm expecting to hear from the vet later on today and I will give you a report.

⋯⋯ ⋅•❧•⋅ ⋯⋯

Charles Guittard

To: Nancy Labastida

Saturday, August 28, 2021, at 10:52 a.m.

Oops. I would be leery of playing Scrabble with you or Password. Did you ever watch Betty White play Password? Women's brains I believe are better suited to contests involving words. I could never beat Pat at Scrabble, and I had the better vocabulary, but it didn't matter at Scrabble. No Scrabble.

Nancy Labastida

To: Charles Guittard

Saturday, August 28, 2021, at 12:57 p.m.

Every single thing you say in this email is absolutely true. We are in good shape and should enjoy our lives in the present. When Fernando died, I told myself, "Nancy, you're still here, and you have to take care of yourself and live your life." That is what I have been doing. As time passes, I really want to live my life happily. Charles, I had nothing like the sadness you went through for so long. Fernando began getting ill with congestive heart failure in 2010. He had a quadruple bypass and came very, very near to death. He was in the ICU for 6 weeks. When he finally came home, the recovery was long, and I was devoted to him and loved taking care of him. We had to move to a one story house, and he had about 7 more years of a pretty good life. We went to Mexico to visit his family every year, and he went to his beloved Blanton Museum once a week and had friends and was loved and doted on by the family. However, during the last 3 or 4 years, it became obvious that he was getting dementia, and that was the hardest to take, as you know. It was crushing, as he had such a brilliant mind. In the end, he went very fast. He was coming home from the hospital in an ambulance to go into hospice at home. He died in our driveway in the ambulance. I really had no idea how I was going to care for him, when hospice wasn't there. At least that first night, we would have been all alone. Everybody thinks he died to save me from that.

You are right, in as much as my life was on hold for eight years. I didn't play tennis during that time, and when I went back, I was shocked at how bad I was!!! Everybody told me to take care of myself, while I was caring for him, so I had my granddaughter come once a week on Thursday afternoon to be with Fernando, so that I could play bridge. He lived for those Thursday afternoons because Claudia was the apple of his eye. I carry on playing tennis; I've accepted that my competitive days are over, even though I'm on a team and do win a couple of matches now and then. I like the exercise and companionship.

I await your big hug at my front door with great anticipation.

Charles Guittard

To: Nancy Labastida

Saturday, August 28, 2021, at 1:02 p.m.

Attached is a screenshot of the Guittards at 1401 South 8th in Waco, Pop and Mama Josie's house. My mother who would have been there has apparently volunteered to take the picture, which is consistent with her personality. My little brother John is at the tip of the spear and I am over and behind his left shoulder. My cousin Steve who has helped me with my book a little is behind and over my left shoulder. Frank Guittard top row far left, and Josie bottom row in black on the far right.

I don't think our family table conversations I would consider today as being terribly interesting, especially to any invited guests who might be present. My grandfather taught history and his two sons were lawyers who could talk about law cases—anyway in retrospect it does not seem terribly fascinating. When the family gathered around the dinner table on special occasions on Desco, my mother took the lead in getting conversations started by throwing out questions as conversation starters or drawing people out on something they might be able to talk about. She also had table games to play after the dessert dishes were cleared away. I suppose they were kind of fun and produced some slight electricity although

I was to learn that Hank, Mary's husband, tended to win anything resembling Trivial Pursuit. My guess is that with your much larger and more diverse family than mine, the dinner conversations would tend naturally to be more entertaining. And we had no entertaining Uncle Joe who kept us all in stitches with his wise-cracks. My other grandfather, Dr. Kee, had his moments when we were at 1819 Morrow in Waco with his various well-worn jokes. His best one was about the young woman who went to the confessional at her local Catholic Church and it went like this:

"Father, I need to confess, I've sinned."
"What is your sin, my child?"
"Father, I've kissed a man."
"Well, say two Hail Mary's and go in peace."

The next day she returns, same priest:

"Father, I've sinned; I must confess."
"And what is your sin?"
"Father, I've kissed a man."
"Well, my child, say five Hail Marys, go in peace, and sin no more."

The next day she returns again, same priest:

"Father, I've sinned. I've kissed a man."
"Kissed a man? Why, my child, do you keep repeating your sin?"
"Oh, no, father, I'm not. It was just one time."
"Well, don't you know your heavenly father has already forgiven you?"
"Oh, I know, Father. I just like to talk about it."

Nancy Labastida

To: Charles Guittard

Saturday, August 28, 2021, at 1:07 p.m.

Yes, you should be very leery. My father used to almost get angry when he would see some of the words that Mom and I used, but they were all in the Scrabble dictionary. Yes, I watched Betty White play "Password!" I also watched my mother, Betty Davis, play Password on television one day, but not with Betty White. The celebrity with whom Mom won $300.00 was Nipsy Russell. Mom and Dad watched "Password" every single day, while they had lunch. Dad always come home for lunch. They never missed it. Well, on a visit they made to me in New York, Mom tried out for "Password" and got selected. She was scheduled to be on a show about a week or so later. She had to postpone her trip back to Dallas. Mom and Dad were to be co-hosts for the monthly (I think monthly) Dance Club group at their house, so Dad went on back home to co-host the party, and Mom stayed with me to be on "Password."

Now, do you remember Truth or Consequences on the radio with Ralph Edwards and the mystery person contest they had? You probably do, knowing that you were our invisible friend in our young lives. We were glued to the radio, especially on Sunday nights.

Charles Guittard

To: Nancy Labastida

Saturday, August 28, 2021, at 1:27 p.m.

Thanks for sharing all of that, especially the dementia part. Pat's mind went but she always knew it was me right up until the last week or so. She couldn't really communicate very well but she still knew it was me and I knew it was her, although an altered or reduced her. She did keep her sense of humor even into the last months of hospice and that was a real blessing. She was never bitter or cursed the fact that she was dying too young. She didn't do the angry Job thing at all, although sometimes she was very sad. I was fortunate to have caregivers like Mary Hayes and caregivers from Faith Hospice who were wonderfully upbeat, caring, and cheerful and we had music therapists, physical therapists, chaplains, RNs, LVNS, and others who would come by. Pat also came to like living at The Reserve; she hated it at first and cried but the caregivers and the music and other programs ameliorated our situation. She made friends easily and was such a brave little trooper and they always wanted to know how she was doing. She was doing her friendly extroverted thing to the end it seemed. And of course being at The Reserve meant that it was convenient to Steve after he came back to the Dallas area. Dementia is very hard to deal with as you know. Although Pat's words and sentences became very limited, you could tell she understood what people said to her and reacted appropriately. She had been such a lively funny sparkplug of a girl the change was very noticeable and it was hard to let her go and tell her it was OK for her to go. But the living have to go on and live and love. Your boyfriend

------------------- ·•◦❧◦•· -------------------

Nancy Labastida

To: Charles Guittard

Saturday, August 28, 2021, at 1:47 p.m.

Oh, Charles, you make me laugh and cry at the same time. Of course, I was shedding tears, while writing about Fernando and again reading your email now, but I also burst out laughing at the way you signed off! My boyfriend. I like the sound of that. I like the idea of being your girlfriend. I love that we can talk freely about Pat and Fernando and use their names with ease. Pat sounds like an absolutely wonderful woman.

Nancy Labastida

To: Charles Guittard

Saturday, August 28, 2021, at 3:04 p.m.

I know you are away from your computer, but nevertheless, I just wanted to quickly answer this email. I think my mother started playing tennis before she met my father, but I think they met on the tennis court. Tennis has been our family sport ever since I can remember. The first hurdle for the kids was to beat our mother. The next hurdle was to beat our father, which was extremely difficult, as he was so tricky with his slices and dices. I don't think I ever beat him, and finally that era was over, when I really concentrated on my tennis. My mother is a very interesting person.

Charles Guittard

To: Nancy Labastida

Saturday, August 28, 2021, at 5:30 p.m.

I had a nice relationship with my mother but it wasn't as tight as those she had with my brother and sister. John and Mary each had different kinds of relationships with her and we can talk about that when we meet. I loved my mother, she thought I was talented and funny, and was always there when I needed her. We weren't enmeshed as the psychiatrists say. To be honest, I could have been a better son and paid more attention to her after I moved to Houston; my brother was often telling me that mother missed talking to me and I would promise to call her. She and I were on very different wavelengths and she was a listener. That doesn't excuse being less attentive to her than I should have been.

I got to thinking about the three Nancys and about my batting average when I played in Nancyland. I only played two games so far in Nancyland and lost both, if we don't count Nancy L–. The first was a sweet Nancy G– in the 7th grade I invited to something after I was in high school at Hillcrest, I can't remember exactly, but her mother said she couldn't go out with me because she was diabetic. Down one.

The second and last Nancy was an attractive and talented Nancy B–, one year behind me in Hillcrest. When I was in SMU Law, there was a social where law students socialized with the Chi Omegas. This was not the kind of thing I was good at but I went and there was Nancy from high school and she was kind of friendly. So I thought, OK, that's good, let's see if she is willing to go out with me. I called and she declined, offering no reason. I suspect she had a boyfriend and just didn't want to use him as an excuse. She later married a doctor who was quite successful, had children, created a great life for herself, and that was that. Down two. So my score with Nancys was a minus two until Classmates.com brought us together. And if I had some wisdom for others interested in playing Nancyland, my advice would be to play as many games as you can and get your batting average up. That would be my advice for those playing in Lindaland, Heatherland, and all the other lands of women.

Charles Guittard

To: Nancy Labastida

Saturday, August 28, 2021, at 5:39 p.m.

The final results are not in, but the Vet says she is predicting liver cancer. Maggie will be staying at the vet at least until Monday.

Nancy Labastida

To: Charles Guittard

Saturday, August 28, 2021, at 5:49 p.m.

I was probably the one child that has always been closest to Mom. Now, Harvey has probably taken my place, since he lives so near and visits often and massages her back and is loyal to the core. My mother and I are the most alike, and I have always enjoyed her company, and I think I understand most of the things about her that bother the other kids. We were mostly on the same wavelength. So much to talk about, Charles.

Nancyland was once a huge field. In my very small first grade mid-term class, there were 4 Nancys. My mother said it was because of Frank Sinatra. He had a daughter about the same time I was born, and her name was Nancy, as was her mother's. I, on the other hand am named after my father's mother whose maiden name was Nancy Virginia Talbot. You can see that my parents named three children after Dad's mother. What was your mother's name? My parents had 4 girls and 4 boys. The oldest was Libby, who died in Austin in 1984 of an asthma attack at the age of 46. She left behind a husband and a 9 year old daughter. I came after Libby and Virginia was born almost 3 years after me. Then Harvey came, just one year after Virginia. Through a series of unique circumstances, my parents adopted a 13 year old girl named Mary Louise, just before we moved to Dallas. After a couple of years in Dallas, Mark was born then Charlotte and Clayton and last was Talbot. Talbot was born when I was 20 and a senior at SMU. He was 2 when I got married and 4 when he became an uncle.

Yes, keep playing in Nancyland until you get it right. I hope your batting average with Nancys goes off the charts now. I have never dated a Charles, so the mystery is still unfolding. I was a Chi Omega at SMU.

Nancy Labastida

To: Charles Guittard

Saturday, August 28, 2021, at 5:55 p.m.

Oh, Charles, that is disappointing news. I send you all my best wishes for the optimum outcome. I hope Maggie is not suffering. I'll be thinking about you and hoping you are doing okay.

***

Charles Guittard

To: Nancy Labastida

Saturday, August 28, 2021, at 6:16 p.m.

If I had only known you back then, you could have at least given me some advice as to how to proceed in Nancyland, with all of its funny turns and quirks, and perhaps how to keep Nancy boots from walking all over me, or any of the other domains inhabited by women, assuming that you and I did not hit off which we probably would have, although not having nearly as much in common as we do now. I never solved the Chi Omegas problem but maybe it was partially a Charles problem—shyness, lack of follow-through and persistence, lack of having enough interesting topics to talk about, or something else. We'll never know. The fact that you were a Chi Omega just proves I may have given up too soon. But I'm happy with where I ended up.

Nancy Labastida

To: Charles Guittard

Saturday, August 28, 2021, at 6:45 p.m.

Hahahaha "Nancy boots from walking all over me!" [Nancy Sinatra song] I love it. I think we do have a lot more in common now, Charles, than we would have had way back in high school and college. We have lived good lives and are ready for whatever comes next. I hope you end up happy in Nancyland and I end up happy, exploring Charlesland.

How long do you plan to stay in Austin? Do you have plans to be with your son and family? I am very easy going. Anything is fine with me. I called Nanette a little while ago to tell her about you. She is very practical. She told me to ask you if you have been vaccinated, but I'm not going to because I'm sure you have.

Charles Guittard

To: Nancy Labastida

Saturday, August 28, 2021, at 7:53 p.m.

I know you think I'm a kind of funny guy after I have launched one absurd remark after another at you and you have taken all my nonsense with good grace—and thank you very much for smiling—but I may not live up to the billing with your family if you have built me up too high. I will be polite and friendly but may come across as uber-serious or stuffy, not an impression I like to give.

Nancy Labastida

To: Charles Guittard

Saturday, August 28, 2021, at 8:04 p.m.

One more thing (I'm the dummy, bridgewise). If Maggie's situation makes it impossible for you to come to Austin, I would consider going to Dallas.

Charles Guittard

To: Nancy Labastida

Saturday, August 28, 2021, at 9:37 p.m.

If plans go in this direction, I will find you a nearby hotel and put it all on my Visa—that way I will get the reward points! And you can stay until you need to go back to Austin. You wouldn't be comfortable at the peanut of an apartment I live in—there's just one bed and a sofa and I don't think that's an ideal arrangement for us at this point. It would be illuminating but depressing I'm afraid. But it will serve well enough for one of our meeting places in Dallas.

Mary, my sister, and John, my brother, both graduated from Hillcrest and Mary also from Franklin. John went on to Amherst and then UT Law and Mary to Hendrix College and North Texas State for her library degree. They've all been very supportive of me in every respect, and I'm sure they would be very curious and excited to meet you and importantly would really like you. With much love, *Charles*

Charles Guittard

To: Nancy Labastida

Saturday, August 28, 2021, at 10:10 p.m.

I'm confident the subject won't be Republican side politics as Mary and Hank and Louise and John K are Dems. John G and Jo are Republicans but John and I have an agreement not to talk politics or make remarks that have a political bite to them. Such remarks would, of course, under Dallas Redbook rules be inappropriate in any event.

The vet is going to call me tomorrow with more info on Maggie.

Charles Guittard

To: Nancy Labastida

Saturday, August 28, 2021, at 11:03 p.m.

The first thing I wanted to say that it has gradually dawned on me what a wonderful writer you are. Really. Sometimes I'm slow but you are always eloquent, interesting, perceptive in your writing, and funny too. So I wanted to get that off my chest before I started using "I" again.

Thank you for all that input on how funny your family is. I do feel a little overwhelmed and somewhat like a wall-flower folding up and going back into the wallpaper just hearing it, but you meant well, I know. If we are able to meet with any of your family, I will just let whatever happens happen. I won't make any notes in advance. God, I'm almost 79, once a board-certified civil trial specialist and a mediator or arbitrator of maybe 400 disputes, talking about making notes. This has got to stop!

BTW, and I know this is inconsistent with all my self-centered talk about my insecurities in the last few emails, but I was at a luncheon for mediators one time with maybe 75 in a hotel dining room. The speaker was a no-show and someone alerted the chair of the program that the speaker had car trouble or whatever. The chair came over to my table, explained the situation, and asked if I would make some remarks for ten minutes and he would get another 1 or 2 guys to do a bit too and the 30 minutes speaker's time would fly by and no one would ask for their luncheon money back. I thought the situation was so odd and so funny and without almost any pressure, so I said yes and had about ten minutes to make some notes. Well, I had a legal pad under the table but I didn't want to use a legal pad to make notes, because my intent was to use the constraints I was under to get some laughs. So I wrote out a few words on the backs of several of those pink sweet and low packets and stood and delivered when the time came. I also reached into my briefcase and pulled out a glossy firm promotional brochure showing a Dallas trial lawyer in cowboy boots and hat standing by his airplane touting all the million-dollar verdicts he said he had obtained. In a way the most satisfying of maybe 50 to 100 talks I gave to a number of groups during that period. I got some laughs too, they sympathized with me, they resented wealthy plaintiffs' lawyers, and wanted to laugh before I even stood behind the rostrum. I don't recommend this way of preparing for talks, however. I just got lucky that day and had an invisible shield around me. Your intimidated boyfriend who will get over it, *Charles*

Nancy Labastida

To: Charles Guittard

Sunday, August 29, 2021, at 8:29 a.m.

I think we could write a book about our one week of emails and how the greetings and endings evolved and all the vast amount of information we have exchanged in just seven days, without ever having seen each other in the past sixty-five years, if we even saw each other ever. Do you remember me from the tennis courts at Northwood or from the halls of Hillcrest?

My thoughts last night, when I couldn't sleep, centered around where we can go in Dallas and what am I going to wear! Also, of course, my thoughts were hoping that we like each other as much in person as we do in emails and that we have chemistry. I feel that we will have chemistry.

Thank you so much for your compliments about my writing. I adore the English language and find it endlessly fascinating. My mother also loved the English language. At times, even when she was in the emergency room, she would correct nurses who got grammar wrong. They would always tell her to lay down, and she would answer, do you want me to lie down. Sometimes that exchange would go back and forth 3 or 4 times. Soon, I would have lean over and tell the nurse that Mom was correcting their grammar. Most nurses laughed and said that they had been talking that way all their lives.

If our initial meeting is in Dallas, I could introduce you to my brother, Mark, who lives in Arlington, but I won't! I'm almost positive that he isn't vaccinated. We always have a lot of fun when we are together. The last time we were all together was at a niece's wedding in Nashville almost 3 years ago, and I was so happy I could hardly contain myself, when we were all in a picture together. The minute the picture taking was over, I burst into tears of sheer emotion, and my eyes are stinging now.

It's interesting to hear about your brother, John, and his wife and also about Mary and her husband. We have so much to talk about regarding our siblings and in-laws. I hate fast driving, and I especially hate tailgating. I never ever tailgate. Fernando hardly ever drove after we were married. We didn't even have a car in New York. We got one in London, but I always drove, even in Europe. I also never wanted to scare him, of course, and he admired my driving, Charles. My father scared me with his driving all those years ago when we drove on two lane roads to tennis tournaments around Texas.

Your mother gave you unusual advice before going off to Baylor. I wish my mother had told me to join groups and get involved in campus activities and make life time memories and study hard to make good grades and don't be boy crazy, but no one told me that. I did study, but not hard enough to get on the Dean's List. I was a Chi Omega, but I didn't get very involved in anything, and dating was my main focus. Sigh. When I drove up to Centenary to drop Clayton off, I gave him the advice I wish I had gotten, except for the boy part. Years later, he thanked me for that. He had a wonderful four years at Centenary and did meet his adorable wife there.

I think you have summarized exactly how I would have felt about your bridge group at Baylor. I would have been impressed by their brilliance, but mystified by their right wing politics. I cannot imagine being insensitive and cruel to the less fortunate. I read *Atlas Shrugged* and the *Fountainhead* and was very, very impressed by both books. Oddly enough, I did not understand that they were right wing books. I had a different take and thought they were about personal responsibility. I was totally intrigued and consumed by both books. For years, I wanted to have a daughter and name her Dominique after one of the main characters. I was obsessed with the name Dominique, even after I got married, until one of my American friends married to a Mexican told me in so many words that it was a bit pretentious to choose a French name to go with a Spanish name. Did I tell you that I lived in Mexico City for the first 7 months of my marriage, and I am fluent, but not bi-lingual, in Spanish?

I hope you love me, when you meet me, my dear, sweet, Charles. With much love, *Nancy*

Charles Guittard

To: Nancy Labastida

Sunday, August 29, 2021, at 9:49 a.m.

That was your best email ever. Now that I am focused on your writing skills, I pay even more attention to the way you write and say things. Perhaps at some point, I can get you to look over my shoulder at my current writing project. I don't want to engage in a heavy rewrite, but my respect for your judgment suggests I need to let you take a look at it and read it over before sending it off to the publisher. Georgette will do her thing with punctuation, spelling, grammar, and a number of other things but feedback from you would likely be a boost for my ego, although since now that I've told you that, I'm afraid you will hold back on constructive criticism. Please don't.

I too had trouble sleeping last night but it was not about what to wear but other things. Like the main thought that kept coming back was a little prayer I kept saying to myself, "Dear Lord, please give me five more years so that I can enjoy this wonderful woman and perhaps add a little something to her life as well." That is so schmaltzy I wasn't even going to tell you that until at a later and appropriate time but it just popped out.

I tried to read *Atlas Shrugged* but got bogged down fairly early and should have read *The Fountainhead* first because I never got to it although I saw the movie with Gary Cooper. Such cold characters. That Nathaniel Branden guy too. I never had any interest in *Anthem*. Somehow I associate the way they think with Madalyn Murray O'Hair, another totally brilliant mind but without a drop of the milk of human kindness. I'm not surprised she was eventually murdered. I heard Madalyn on the radio one time debate Wally Amos Criswell, First Baptist pastor in Dallas, I'm sure you remember him; he perpetually wept during his sermons. By the way, he told me one time that he took history from my grandfather at Baylor. I doubt Frank Guittard would have been a fan of W.A.; he certainly would have been put off by his perpetual weeping during the delivery of sermons.

I'm not sure if we had been high school sweethearts we would have a better story; a longer one, sure. We are who we are today because of the paths we have taken and the experiences we have had, for good or for bad. Our lives have not all been about picnics and roses and there have been real hard times too. Though a lot of our experiences and background are similar, the diversity is part of the secret sauce that makes me love you. My college roommate Larry A— I think had it wrong; he said he was looking for a girl whose interests were identical to his own. I remember when he met his wife Robbie, he gave her what he called "the sense of life test" which was to play a record by the Up with People Group and get her reaction. If she reacted positively, then that was a good sign. She passed the test and they got married. He asked my father to officiate and I prepared the words for my father to read. Since Larry was an objectivist, he was an atheist. So I cleverly took the Methodist order of service, typed it up, and excised the words, God and Christ, and Holy Ghost, and so on throughout. They were married in the French Room of the Adolphus and it was tony but very odd. Maybe five years later they divorced. He said the problem was she wanted an open marriage. I suspect she was just worn out being married to Larry who was very intense with all of his objectivist nonsense.

To answer your question about how I remember you, I'm not exactly sure, but I'm positive I remember that you were a tennis player at Hillcrest because of your picture in the annual. Love, your hungry and sleepy *Charles*

Charles Guittard

To: Nancy Labastida

Sunday, August 29, 2021, at 9:58 a.m.

I wasn't afraid of my father although I was rather nervous around him because neither he nor I were very willing to share our feelings with each other. He was a shy guy who accomplished a lot with Mother's support and his own inherent will to succeed. He was a brilliant writer, first in his law class like your father, and could have corrected the King James language if given the chance. As a speaker, he was eloquent but did not speak smoothly. Although he tried cases, his specialty was appellate work which was 90 percent about research and writing and 10 percent about oral argument.

Charles Guittard

To: Nancy Labastida

Sunday, August 29, 2021, at 11:42 a.m.

It is healthy. I get the Salata mix, arugula, kale, spinach, then broccoli, carrots, mushrooms, chickpeas, black beans, blueberries, strawberries, red grapes, watermelon chunks, fresh herb vinaigrette, pumpkin seeds, cranberries, and a fruit drink. I skip the croissant and pita pieces, they are tasty, but I'm trying to reduce caloric intake. Oh, I also had a chunk of salmon for four bucks and get them to crunch it up for me. The day before yesterday I went to La Madeline's and had a salad with salmon and it was not as good, or as pricey, as Salata. The soups are also good but I don't do them anymore.

Also, please tell me how to pronounce Labastida. I don't want my kin started off wrong and then they never get it right after that. I never took Spanish and I'm afraid to guess. I can pronounce Davis.

Nancy Labastida

To: Charles Guittard

Sunday, August 29, 2021, at 9:57 p.m.

Charles, I hope your sons will not think you are koo koo, when they see my picture. You are on my mind, and I miss you, even though I have never been with you. On the other hand, I feel like you are my companion all day long.

Charles Guittard

To: Nancy Labastida

Monday, August 30, 2021, at 9:40 a.m.

I tried Steve again for the third time and left a longer voice mail message: "Hey, Steve, call me. You are not the only one who has a girlfriend. I will give you details if you call me."

Charles Guittard

To: Nancy Labastida

Monday, August 30, 2021, at 4:19 p.m.

Never in my wildest dreams would I have imagined one day sitting down with three members [Nancy, Harvey, and Virginia] of the famous Davis tennis family, any one of whom could have creamed me playing left-handed. I will bring my newest and fanciest set of sweatpants (tri-color down the pants legs) plus a blue blazer for the event. So I hope it will be a fairly casual affair and location. And not too noisy so I can hear the words coming out of the mouths of all of us. If I need to be fancier than this, I trust you will let me know.

Nancy Labastida

To: Charles Guittard

Monday, August 30, 2021, at 5:03 p.m.

Charles, I booked your room for 3 nights. I'll send the other reservation. Any room can be cancelled. I'm a member of the rewards program, so I think I got a bit of a discount. It's been a while since I have been to a La Quinta. You and I can spend a lot of time at my house, looking at annuals and my funny, messy scrapbook of my early tennis days and watching the U.S. Open and playing Scrabble and brushing up on bridge. It will be fun to go out to Lakeway. It's a nice drive.

Charles Guittard

To: Nancy Labastida

Monday, August 30, 2021, at 6:42 p.m.

I just got a call from the Vet who says Maggie is in seriously bad shape and may not survive the night. She deteriorated in her condition dramatically in the last hour. In a few minutes I'm going to go back to Citivet and spend some time with her. I'm guessing she will be euthanized tomorrow or the next day. I am so glad I took her to the Vet on Friday to get some care at least before she leaves me.

Charles Guittard

To: Nancy Labastida

Tuesday, August 31, 2021, at 7:00 a.m.

I hope I have not been running you too ragged with all of these emails and giddy shows of affection over the past 8 or 9 days. It has been a long time since I have been in a conversation with a woman. In person, I am not that clever correspondent I have tried to be to capture your interest and then your heart but a much more ordinary guy who would have liked to have been a writer but ended up enrolling in law school and becoming a mediator. So I am going to do my best to stop trying to be clever and humorous and be more of the person I am normally.

In short, I want to go down an easy road with you and I want you to feel easy with me. I could hear myself listening to you last night and trying to be ready with my next story. So I am going to stop doing that I hope. I won't be trying to impress Virginia, Harvey or Gayle or put on a show in order to come out of my shell. I want to find that easy street with you. I don't want to worry about lulls in the conversation or for you to worry about them either. Peace and quiet and holding hands really sound good to me. There is nothing too humorous in this email so I'm off to a good start this morning.

Nancy Labastida

To: Charles Guittard

Tuesday, August 31, 2021, at 7:14 a.m.

I love that you have opened yourself to me in this email. In the beginning of any relationship, both parties are trying to impress each other. Sometimes that trying to be clever and charming act lasts for a long time, and it's not real. I'm glad you feel you want to show me the real you, which I suspect is humorous, but mostly kind and considerate and caring. Let's just both be ourselves when we finally meet and get to know each other sincerely. I'm glad that you won't be trying to impress Harvey and Virginia; they would notice. We are all down to earth sort of people. Bill is just an easy-going lovely man. I hope he brings his guitar. I'll tell Virginia to tell him to bring it.

By the way, your stories are very interesting. Telling each other the important stories in our lives are what we are doing now. We are both so full of stories and life experiences. I know that I just want to tell you everything, and I hope you feel the same way about me.

Charles Guittard

To: Nancy Labastida

Tuesday, August 31, 2021, at 9:01 a.m.

Just learned that dear Maggie passed away last night peacefully not long after I visited with her. I am going to go by the Vet's place and finish up.

Nancy Labastida

To: Charles Guittard

Tuesday, August 31, 2021, at 11:55 a.m.

Well, it would be fun and interesting for me to hear your bucket list. I haven't had a bucket list, but my life has changed in the last week or so, so it will be a good topic. I have been thinking of a trip we could take, however it's all about me. I was thinking of a Davis sibling tour, starting in Houston with Charlotte and then Lake Charles with Clayton. Then I'd like to take a little detour to Florida to visit my new best friend (well before you became my new best friend), Judy Pressley, who was in my class at Hillcrest. You can look her up. Judy and I have become very, very close in the last year. Then on to Charlotte, NC to visit Talbot. I came to this idea only after trying to think of where I would like to go in the US, and I remembered that I would like to go to Charleston, SC, so that would be the last stop. Another dreamy trip for me would be a train trip. Now, I am remembering places where I would like to go - the last one is Alaska. Everyone is going there, though, so it seems almost like a cliche. Where would you like to go?

Charles Guittard

To: Nancy Labastida

Tuesday, August 31, 2021, at 4:46 p.m.

Just to let you know a little about the things I'm bringing: the book illustrations; some Hillcrest annuals; some Baylor annuals; a few other items. I'm not bringing any Pat & Charles scrapbooks. There is a lot of that at the Sparkman/Hillcrest website including both a slide show of a lot of photos and a video of the memorial service if you want to look at any of that before I get there. I have watched it all many times. Mary Hayes is the first or second speaker–I forget—and I think she stole the show. She got there a few minutes late and we delayed starting until she got there, dressed to the 9s and ready to roll.

You must have a ton of stuff, and I'm sure it's not practical or desirable to try to go thru much of it in our get-acquainted session. Just whatever you would like to share on our first visit about you especially, your family, your days with Fernando, or whatever.

Charles Guittard

To: Nancy Labastida

Tuesday, August 31, 2021, at 7:07 p.m.

Please don't tell your bridge buddies or anyone I'm bringing baby pictures—that is going to sound pretty narcissistic and weird, me thinking anyone would even want to see them, especially on our first meeting! How many first "dates" can you think of where someone brought their baby pictures along!!! The more I think about it, the goosier I'm getting about bringing them, thinking stories are going to spread and I will be saddled with those stories forever. Every time I enter a room, people will start smiling at nothing in particular.

Charles Guittard

To: Nancy Labastida

Tuesday, August 31, 2021, at 9:00 p.m.

Sometimes I walk around The Reserve in the parking lot but if it's still light, I walk around the beautiful lake at the T Boone Pickens Hospice Center. It is a hidden jewel with multiple ways to proceed and double back. Hardly any dog doo on the paths and not many people. If we are able to get you up here, you can walk with me. It's not strenuous the way I do it but I have an oximeter to monitor my pulse and oxygen numbers and I try to follow the advice of my PT Lara McCrary who I generally see on Wednesday mornings. We don't always talk health; sometimes we talk about how Charles is doing and I tell her just enough to keep her curiosity up.

Nancy Labastida

To: Charles Guittard

Wednesday, September 1, 2021, at 1:44 p.m.

Charles, I was working in the DPL [Dallas Public Library], when John Kennedy was killed. I saw him and Jackie as they began the fateful drive down Elm Street. The next two days, I just stood in a window in the corner of the children's room, where I worked and watched as all the news vans and reporters were swarming that building [Police Courts Building catty-cornered to the DPL], waiting for Lee Harvey Oswald to be transferred [to the Dallas County Courthouse]. Nobody came to the library that day, and we were all in shock. Then on Sunday, I went to church with my mother for the first time in many years, and the priest (Episcopal) announced that Oswald had been killed. My father was home and saw it live on television. Oh, and my father was at the lunch, waiting for the arrival of Kennedy that dreadful day in November, 1963. I left the DPL in January, 1964 to get married.

Again, we are so alike. I saw the movie The Story of Will Rogers, as quite a young girl and was hooked for life on him. I was blown away completely because I don't think I knew much about him until I saw that movie.

Actually, maybe I am [now] the matriarch. I know all the family history, like birthdays, including the year, and I have everybody's address and phone number. The others are always asking for information. The younger ones are quite content with their position in the family. Talbot almost makes a career of being the way youngest of 8. He says he's an only child with 7 older brothers and sisters. We are all pretty confident in our positions. In Mexico, it is expected that the oldest brother will be the patriarch, when the father dies. Fernando was the oldest of 5 brothers and had a much younger sister, but he was never the patriarch type.

Nancy Labastida

To: Charles Guittard

Wednesday, September 1, 2021, at 3:10 p.m.

I think you found me first on Classmates and left a remark about me. Then you sent me a friend request on Facebook. I joined Classmates almost the minute I got [returned] to the states. I was hungry to find old friends. Facebook is also a wonderful tool for finding old friends. There are always chance meetings, so we could have met, had I not married and left Dallas forever (except for a multitude of visits) in 1964. I don't want us to not cherish the lives we have had up until now, but the future holds the possibility of great and unexpected joy. I'm glad that you think the dreamy concept of soulmates is poppycock, because I always feel a little jealous when people say they are with their soulmate.

<hr />

Nancy Labastida

To: Charles Guittard

Wednesday, September 1, 2021, at 3:35 p.m.

On Classmates you left exactly those remarks: attractive and athletic. I think I might have discovered that you went to SMU law school on Classmates, so when we became friends on FB, I messaged you and asked you if you knew my father, and that's how it all began. I must leave now and go to my gym session.

Charles Guittard

To: Nancy Labastida

Wednesday, September 1, 2021, at 6:20 p.m.

Nice. Some jitters here but excited to be going to Austin to meet you finally.

Nancy Labastida

To: Charles Guittard

Wednesday, September 1, 2021, at 6:23 p.m.

Jitters are to be expected with both of us. I can hardly wait to meet you. It made me smile to write that, since I feel I know you already.

Nancy Labastida

To: Charles Guittard

Wednesday, September 1, 2021, at 7:15 p.m.

Well, it might come up with me. I often fear I talk too much. Almost time for the bridge tournament. It's time to log on.

Charles Guittard

To: Nancy Labastida

Thursday, September 2, 2021, at 4:28 a.m.

OK, I can't sleep. I give up. My mind is just racing. Will go back to bed when my brain slows down. I think Armando's wife's name was Ann. Does that ring a bell? A pleasant-looking blonde...From Northwood's pool area I hear an African-American woman's voice saying, "Billy Jordan, Billy Jordan, your order's ready." Apparently, Billy Jordan doesn't pick up his order immediately, and I hear the same voice again and saying the same thing...Armando smoking his pipe and talking about how great Bobby Riggs was...The framed picture of Pancho Segura on the clubhouse wall. Armando stringing rackets...Wayne Sabin saying Harvey Jr. could give me a good game...The dining room buffet on Sundays and Northwood's special salad dressing...A tennis player younger than I but better named Carl Gregory. Carl had lost some fingers on perhaps his left hand. He could still beat me...A neighbor of mine wanting to play at Northwood, but I never invited him to play and regretted it. He later died in a car crash with his wife...

Hitting golf balls off the driving range and getting where I could do it pretty well...Decades later going to a commercial driving range on Park Lane, paying for a bag of balls, and not being able to hit a single solid shot. Either I sliced it, hooked it, or shanked it...Playing Sousaphone in the beginning band at HPJr. under director Charles Thomas...Practicing after school on a school tuba until I was good enough to qualify for the main band when I would have one of those cool uniforms ...Transferring to Hillcrest where I would play Sousaphone one or two years while taking trombone lessons from Art Wilson, 1st chair, Dallas Symphony

Orchestra...Playing at a very cold football game at Franklin Field where the metal mouthpieces of horn players were sticking to their lips...Having an old uniform issued to me at Hillcrest which was really almost worn-out but it was the first uniform I ever wore and I thought it was really cool...Sue K– who my New York cousin Steve dated when he was in the D.A.' s office in Dallas...Her younger sister, who was a friend of Mary G–...Dick Chaplin's dance studio and the time I let a girl down on her birthday...Playing in the orchestra for *Oklahoma*, one of my greatest experiences at Hillcrest...Taking first place at the debate tournament in south Texas and beating a team from Houston by a 4-1 decision...Receiving a summa cum laude ribbon from my Latin teacher Mrs. Hamilton...Maxyne Cammack, my algebra teacher, a real card, a golfer, and in the same Single Adult Class at Highland Park Methodist I was in. Maybe I can go back to sleep now

[*Nancy's note: Your reference above to the words "Billy Jordan, Billy Jordan..." at Northwood Club's poolside snack bar blew me away. After all the coincidences we've already talked about, this coincidence reaches deeply into this bit of Davis family folklore: while the older Davis children were at the pool every day in the summer, they would hear those magical words, "Harvey Davis, Harvey Davis, your order is ready," maybe only once a month. In those days money was more precious than it was by the time that Talbot, the last of our clan, showed up. Talbot could order a hamburger whenever he wanted, and, to this day, can repeat those words with the proper emphasis and drawl. The fact that his older siblings had to ask for special permission to order a poolside hamburger and Talbot never did, still makes us all chuckle.*]

Charles Guittard

To: Nancy Labastida

Thursday, September 2, 2021, at 5:09 a.m.

Oh, gosh, Nancy, you are not supposed to be up but resting and getting really mellow. I can see your point about the IPad; maybe you will let me play with yours a little. I am not technological at all. I had several books on grieving; the best one was a kind of a grieving by the numbers, formulaic but effective. I remember I wrote out a final message to Pat and took Maggie to a park on Campbell Road and started to give my little speech into a tape recorder when I was interrupted by an elderly woman who wanted to approach Maggie and pet her. I curtly but I hope politely declined. The next day feeling bad about being rude to this very old woman, I drove back over there, up and down nearby neighborhood streets, spotted her, pulled up in front of her house, she saw me and walked over to my door, and I explained to her why I had not been very friendly. She seemed to accept my explanation. It was a great little book and planning and delivering a final message to Pat did me a world of good. I did the same thing with Maggie but I just did it impromptu without a tape recorder.

I'm still doing my gratitude journal to ward off feeling down. I don't have bouts of depression but without Pat and Mary [Hayes] and now Maggie every day and all of those hospice people coming in and out and living as a book-writing hermit despite lunches every week with friends, I still am missing human contact, but it's not just any contact I miss, but something special like NANCY. When the Nancy thing popped up, it was very welcome since I was in this place where I was partly out in the world but partly in this semi-hermit place.

Once the book is done and I'm not too far away from the end of the road now that I have an editor, then the world is going to open up a lot more for me. I don't have any more big writing projects in mind or even medium-sized projects I want to do, although a small project here or there might come up. I want to enjoy my grandchildren and friends including new friends, movies, opera, symphony, and other forms of music, art galleries, tennis matches, football games, good food at interesting places, other cities including places around Texas, cruises, train trips, going to Whole Foods, and brushing up on bridge and playing bridge again, and almost anything if I can do it with the person I love.

As to falling asleep at opera or symphony, yes as to symphony, no as to opera. I love opera and the Met simulcasts. You must go to one with me. It is such an incredible experience and I enjoy the simulcasts in a way I never enjoyed live performances—I know that sounds strange, but I enjoy the interviews with cast members right before they sing their death arias, interviews with costume designers, and other add-ons during intermissions.

Nancy Labastida

To: Charles Guittard

Thursday, September 2, 2021, at 4:30 p.m.

I was a little confused and bemused at the beginning of our now legendary correspondence, but you won me over by your humor, kindness, sweetness and openness. People always say to watch out for any man who shows interest, because they are either interested in a "purse or a nurse," but that is the last thing I have to worry me. My girlfriends just left. It got pretty loud and rowdy at the end with all of them making jokes and remarks about our meeting. Some of them want to take their daily walk along my street at around 6:00 and feign innocence. I should say that I'll put a white flag in front if it's okay and a red one, if it's not. Did I tell you that we play for money? I came in second and won $15.00.

Charles Guittard

To: Nancy Labastida

Thursday, September 2, 2021, at 5:19 p.m.

No, I didn't know you played for money, just for glory and master's points. I am glad you are adding to your savings. If you play for money, then that is proof you are not just fooling around but are a real professional and that is impressive. I used to play for money too but I don't think I ever won as much as $15. That's real money and it will spend.

I hadn't heard the line about "purse or a nurse." Hopefully, neither of those is my motivation. Honestly, we never know when we might need a nurse, as life and health are so uncertain. I've been a caregiver and nurse to Pat since 2013 in gradual phases and of course, would be willing to do the same for you if we really do hit it off in person and become partners. But I believe I can categorically rule out "purse." I'm not surprised that the purse or nurse thing has at least passed through your mind; that would seem to be a healthy question to ask. I know your sisters, children, and your family must be very protective of you and watch what you do and who you spend time with. I am happy that I have apparently passed the initial inspection without even seeing me or meeting me which must mean they have a lot of confidence in your judgment, at least to this point. The circumstances of our connection are unusual, particularly the rate of acceleration, and do bear watching. I'm sure you and I are both aware of this and realize that what is going on is surprising and should be looked at carefully before any decisions are made. Lara, who is very supportive of me and now you, said there have been studies of people who looked up their old classmates on Facebook, connected or got married, and regretted it. I haven't seen the studies but it makes sense. Mary didn't know whether to gasp or laugh when I told her I had never met you, but she laughed. Assuming it pans out for us in some fashion, we certainly have a good story to tell.

Your remark about your friends walking around your house at 6 p.m. shows that I was right to insist on a promise about baby pictures. You've heard that pop song "Cathy's Clown"? A man can only take so much and then he spontaneously combusts and is no more.

Charles Guittard

To: Nancy Labastida

Thursday, September 2, 2021, at 5:51 p.m.

I know you are easy-going and we will have a good time. I'm sure though you from moment to moment may say to yourself "I feel calm, I feel mellow," it's more human to feel jittery. I think all of our sharing to this point has let a lot of tension out of the balloon. There is such a long list of questions you and I have already answered about each other and we have already reached out to nearly all of our family members who have all said, "you go guy" or "you go gal." Moreover, it seems I've told you more about myself and my family than I have ever told anyone. Pat and I had a very nice relationship where sharing was concerned, but yours and mine has been intensive, unusual hyper-sharing and it has felt very natural. So I am really looking forward to that very first moment when we see each other face to face. That will be a moment to remember, dear Nancy.

Charles Guittard

To: Nancy Labastida

Thursday, September 2, 2021, at 6:53 p.m.

One of my traits you may have guessed already is that if I seem somewhat impulsive—I suppose I am. Still, I am a bit of an over-preparer. I am bringing a bunch of stuff but I don't want anyone to think I'm moving in so I' m working on consolidating, perhaps leaving some of this stuff at the hotel. Ten boxes being transported into your house would send the wrong signal to the neighbors.

I have left out all that stuff about my life as a lawyer and spared you from all that. I am not ashamed of having been an attorney, but that is not who I am now, and it was always something of a choice of occupation by default anyway. Love, your nutty boyfriend...

———◦✦◦———

Charles Guittard

To: Nancy Labastida

Thursday, September 2, 2021, at 7:17 p.m.

I'm doubting that anyone anywhere has done anything comparable to what we are doing this weekend, when you consider the way time has been compressed for us and each email has led to the next email. Frank Guittard rushed Josie Glenn pretty hard and their letters are in my last book; they will definitely make you smile. I don't consider that either of us is rushing the other, but only seizing upon the opportunity to explore the obvious attraction attended by a lot of good feeling for each other going in.

"TWO FOR THE SHOW": MEETING IN PERSON

Nancy Labastida

To: Charles Guittard

Friday, September 3, 2021, at 7:06 a.m.

Good morning, Charles. I was up a couple of times during the night, but mostly I slept well. I got up way too early, though. You're so funny, checking your mail to see if you have an email from me and then being glad that you don't. You will be on my mind more than ever today, as you drive to Austin and stop at the Turkey Shop. I will be happy when I hear from you. Drive carefully. I know it's a cliche, but it always helps me when a loved one tells me that before I embark on a road trip; it stays in my head during the drive.

Nancy Labastida

To: Charles Guittard

Monday, September 6, 2021, at 2:33 p.m.

I wanted you to be greeted by an email from me, when you get home. I had a beautiful time with you this weekend. Everything was just about perfect. I'll never forget our last night together. I love you,
Nancy

Charles Guittard

To: Nancy Labastida

Monday, September 6, 2021, at 3:51 p.m.

The only thing that wasn't 100 percent was the shower, and we eventually got it to work! Hate to say it because I don't want you to worry about me or cut back on our late and early hours with each other, but I caught my head bobbing and snapping back a few times on the drive back. Not to worry though—I kept myself reasonably alert by changing the radio station to country and western ballads.

You are just so precious to me. I really have no hard and fast desires for you and me except to be a committed couple. I may be coming across as very impulsive, but overall my MO is to think things through and not act on the first impulse. One goal I have is to live with you because I hurt without you; where and when is to be decided and I am very flexible. I know this is something that can't be rushed and there are other people and issues to be thought through.

Nancy Labastida

To: Charles Guittard

Monday, September 6, 2021, at 5:12 p.m.

I'm so glad to hear that you made it home safely, and I hope you have had a nice nap. As soon as bridge was finished, and I talked to you on the phone, I took a nap for about an hour. It felt so good, but my bed seems different to me now. I'm going to be lonely. Charles, when you come back to Austin, we can talk more seriously about your moving in with me.

Charles Guittard

To: Nancy Labastida

Monday, September 6, 2021, at 6:36 p.m.

I just finished two hours of horizontal and feel much better. Although looking forward to hearing from you, I had no trouble falling asleep. That must be for no other reason than I was so tired that even thinking about you was not keeping me awake. I'm glad you will be thinking about my moving in at some point.

Charles Guittard

To: Nancy Labastida

Tuesday, September 7, 2021, at 3:47 a.m.

First time up. Turkey Shop sandwich yesterday really good. Katie's birthday September 15. Ran a big load of laundry last night but haven't put it in the drier yet. I need a light bulb for my office closet. I really should fold all those clean clothes on my bed. It's about time to do my taxes; it won't be hard to do. I need to check in with Georgette and see how she is coming on her current editing job. I only did one or two turns walking around the hospice park last night. I should find my oximeter and go out early this morning. Those deer were really something. Schenken. That was another system. I think I had a book explaining Schenken but never read it.

I have mixed feelings about Novak. I want him to be the new leader in Slams and get ahead of Nadal and Federer. I don't like the "wolf" side—or maybe it's just scary. McEnroe's hostility was just that of a bad little boy who might actually grow up one day. Novak's is something different. But I still like Novak because his story is good for tennis and he is an amazing guy. I never liked Ilie Nastase.

Nancy Labastida

To: Charles Guittard

Tuesday, September 7, 2021, at 7:23 a.m.

Good morning, my sweet man. I was delighted to find this email waiting for me, but I did want to have my coffee and scrambled eggs with tomato slices before answering. I slept like a baby last night. Don't know about the snoring. Sigh, I'm so glad your Turkey Shop sandwich was all that you expected, especially since the first one ended up in the trash.

I did a big load of laundry, too, washed and dried. There were sheets that yet have not gone back on the bed and towels that are not yet folded or hung on pegs. I gave myself permission to wait until today, when I would have recovered from late nights and early mornings. Oddly enough, I need a new light bulb, also. It's one in the kitchen, although I'm enjoying the new feeling of different lighting because of one less light bulb shining.

Schenken is a very sophisticated [bridge bidding] system and mostly used by smarty pants players who want to intimidate opponents and accumulate massive amounts of master points. We will not be using it! I have very mixed emotions about Novak, and I do not want him to break all [tennis] records, although he will say all the right things in his interviews, if he does. Basically, he is a nice and witty guy, but still..... I never liked Nastase either. I hated his hair and his unacceptable behavior. It was compelling to watch him, but I thought his antics were unfair and unsportsmanlike.

Today, I will either take a walk or go on the treadmill, after I read the paper that arrived this morning, thankfully. I'm going to finally go to the grocery store. I'm happy that I don't have my regular Tuesday morning bridge game with my London friends, as I really need the time for my above mentioned activities. I do have my regular game with Austin friends today at 1:00-4:00. I will get very sleepy during the game, but will have to fight off sleep. We will be chatting on the phone. Your name just might arise. Then I have a bridge tournament tonight. You will be in my heart and in my mind all the time. When I type in C in the To space for an email, I have to be careful not to send the email to Charlotte or my good friend, Charlsa, whose father was a Charles. With all my love, *Nancy*

Nancy Labastida

To: Charles Guittard

Tuesday, September 7, 2021, at 8:56 a.m.

You are so sweet to be fighting off feelings of anxiety or jealousy about Fernando, Jr. Hahaha. He is a very affable and cheerful person. It's hard to explain him; you will just have to meet him. He wouldn't dream of opposing our relationship, unless he sensed something sinister about you, which he won't do.

He is open and boyish and a people person. It's Nanette you need to fear. Now, I've gone and added new anxieties for you. I'll make sure you meet her next time.

Charles Guittard

To: Nancy Labastida

Tuesday, September 7, 2021, at 9:23 a.m.

Your remarks about Fernando helped. I never dreamed Nanette might be someone to fear. It may not matter if all of my family and your bridge club, Harvey, Virginia and all of your buddies out there in tennisland think I'm OK, if Fernando or Nanette has a problem. Note to file: Charles, you don't want to appear to be rushing Nancy too much; what you think is so charming and romantic may not go down well with F or Nanette. BTW, I just realized that Nanette is a play on your name! I also remember my uncle wasn't interested in Frank Guittard [my grandfather] getting remarried to Josie, and said, "Oh, Pop, why would you want to go out and do that for? We were doing pretty good." Of course, my uncle was only 12 at the time and my father was 4. So you will need to tell me more about Nanette and her children. Also more about Fernando, what he does for a living, and more about his kids. If we can get to talking about kids and grandkids, I think we are home-free. Your doting boyfriend, *Charles*

Nancy Labastida

To: Charles Guittard

Tuesday, September 7, 2021, at 12:23 p.m.

I just told all my siblings about you. Harvey sent out an invitation to a Davis Sibling Zoom this weekend. I said I would try, but I would be in Santa Fe. I also said that if he postponed the Zoom for a week, they might meet the new man in my life and proceeded to tell them a bit about you and us. I featured the words Northwood and Hillcrest, so there would be any suspicions about you. Talbot wrote back: WHAT.THE. HELL!!! I know he loves it, though. Clayton wrote back: "How fun! Good for you." I haven't heard from Mark yet. They are the only ones who were still in the dark. I'm pretty sure I will hear more from Talbot.

Whew! I've made the bed. Now, I am watching Medvedev slaughter his opponent. I will watch the ladies match next with the mute button on, as I will be playing bridge and talking on the phone.

Charles Guittard

To: Nancy Labastida

Tuesday, September 7, 2021, at 3:31 p.m.

I was expecting my fortune at Panda Express would be the usual "be happy in p.m." and so was pleasantly surprised when it said: "A THRILLING TIME IS IN YOUR IMMEDIATE FUTURE." That sounds pretty good but it also would been apt for our weekend.

Nancy Labastida

To: Charles Guittard

Tuesday, September 7, 2021, at 4:40 p.m.

Charles, I'll just quote them here. Clayton: How fun! Good for you. Me: It's all fun. That's one of the main points! Virginia: He's really nice, too. Clayton: He damn well better be. Talbot: It would be a miscarriage of justice if he wasn't. That's it. Nothing from Mark. I've talked on the phone extensively with Charlotte and Harvey.

Charles Guittard

To: Nancy Labastida

Tuesday, September 7, 2021, at 5:04 p.m.

After I met you, I was started to get pretty dissatisfied with living here in Dallas. Before meeting you, I was OK. I hope living together, whenever we are able to pull that off, will work for us. I really have no doubts, as long as our people or nearly all of our people are on board—it doesn't have to be 100 percent—but that would be nice and it looks like all of that is coming right along. I don't want to drive you or me crazy emailing you. Living together may be the only answer. Maybe if I took a melatonin in the morning it would calm me down a little. I'll ask Lara what she advises.

<hr />

Nancy Labastida

To: Charles Guittard

Tuesday, September 7, 2021, at 5:39 p.m.

The only doubts I have about living together is having some alone time, which I cherish, also being able to play my bridge games. I think I will have to cut back. My friends are afraid they will lose me, so I will HAVE to play my Thursday afternoon bridge. All that will be worked out, I have no doubt. I am wondering where you will have your computer, which you must have. We will work that out with Fernando's help, I hope.

Charles, you do not drive me crazy with emailing. Your emails are an essential part of my day. I'd be lonelier without them. I don't know, but I think if you take melatonin in the morning, you will be tired all day rather than calmed down. Who knows? Not me, but you are fine just the way you are, as Mr. Rogers would say.

Charles Guittard

To: Nancy Labastida

Tuesday, September 7, 2021, at 6:01 p.m.

You're having alone time is a given. When I get on the computer working on writing or reading a book, I can always be interrupted but the time can pass rather quickly sometimes when I get wrapped up in something sometimes and time can get by me. If you did not have your bridge and tennis friends, then I would feel like it was up to me to keep you entertained and keep you from feeling lonely. Neither you nor I is/are the clingy type. Sometimes I will want to go to a movie you have no interest in or do something that doesn't work with your schedule on a particular day. And your bridge games and tennis games are you; I love to hear your stories. No bridge, no tennis, you may run out of stories, at least out of fresh stories. And we both will have friends and appointments in Austin to do by ourselves.

Nancy Labastida

To: Charles Guittard

Tuesday, September 7, 2021, at 6:46 p.m.

You have said all the right things. I have been saying that I would never live with another man, that it would be the last thing I would ever want to do, but now I am wondering why I ever thought that. I love our current clinginess; it's thrilling for me. I love that you say that you are so intoxicated with me that you can't focus on other things. That makes me feel loved and wanted in all the right ways.

Charles Guittard

To: Nancy Labastida

Tuesday, September 7, 2021, at 7:11 p.m.

For you to even thought you would never live with another man, that would have been such a waste.

* * *

Nancy Labastida

To: Charles Guittard

Tuesday, September 7, 2021, at 7:19 p.m.

Charles, I had not met you, when I said I would never live with another man.

* * *

Charles Guittard

To: Nancy Labastida

Tuesday, September 7, 2021, at 10:05 p.m.

I'm sure I will have to come up with another writing project after I finish the current one. So we can talk about writing one together with me way in the background since arguably it would be your story, but fictionalized. We can include the fun incidents, etc. from your story plus make up the rest including some stuff that is really weird or really funny or really tragic. Would be a hoot even if you only made two bucks in royalty and it would become part of your family's story thing. "Majoring in the Minor Suits: A Story of Life at the Bridge Table and the Desperate Struggle for Masters' Points," by Nancy Davis Labastida

———————— ⋅•✦✐•⋅ ————————

Charles Guittard

To: Nancy Labastida

Wednesday, September 8, 2021, at 10:04 p.m.

I love you. Such a nice and honest email. I know your life was working for you, and I, on the other hand, have suffered a more recent great loss of a spouse. I have substantially recovered, and then Maggie died, and that figures into all of this, plus the fact that working on my book has meant that I live more monastically than you. To some extent, it's hard to compare my relationships, including my two marriages, arising at different times and under different circumstances. But my relationship with you is very special, our communication, closeness, and chemistry in particular, and currently I am happier than I have ever been.

Whew! That was pretty heavy. My prior email about needing you arose from the fact, you might be interested to know, the words of the schmaltzy *Unchained Melody* were still going through my head, and the singer is making very clear not only that he/she misses his beloved person, loves her, but that he needs her. So that's what got me wondering whether I was doing as well in my message to my Nancy as he did to his special person. OK, what time do you have to leave for the airport tomorrow? I want to tell you goodbye before you leave.

Nancy Labastida

To: Charles Guittard

Wednesday, September 8, 2021, at 10:22 p.m.

I've been thinking more ever since I answered your previous email, if I need you. I'm sure that if you were to leave me, I would need you desperately. I've also been thinking about our communication, and I know that I have never been as close to anyone, as I am to you. I love our talking we did in on Monday morning. You are so open and honest, that I am charmed by you and drawn to you and want to be with you. Yes, we have only just begun. I feel like I would never have to wait until you are in a good mood to tell you something or worry about telling you something. I think I could wake you up in the middle of the night to tell you something, and you would not be mad, but would listen and would care. It is the most comforting and cozy feeling to be with a man like you. I care very, very deeply for you. I never imagined myself talking this way, Charles.

Charles Guittard

To: Nancy Labastida

Thursday, September 9, 2021, at 2:31 a.m.

I got to thinking a few minutes ago as I was on the way to the john, that I hope you didn't feel pressured last night to let me see your cards before you were really ready to, and that you feel OK with the things you said. I accept all of it as completely sincere because it came from you. Still, I thought Nancy is so sweet and so careful not to hurt my feelings, maybe she thought I was about to leave her if I didn't hear the word "need." That was not the case at all although I admit to being somewhat heartened when your last emails came through. I have admitted that I am needy somewhere but I don't want to use it as a shield from the truth. If you had not said those affirming things later, I would have hung in there anyway—*after all, faint heart neer gets fair lady*—and given the situation time to work its way through in my favor. Although I could not have said in our case that our feelings were exactly reciprocal, I would have had enough faith in me—don't ask me why because I couldn't tell you—and in us that they eventually would have been. Gosh, that is such an egotistical thing to say, but eventually, I thought you would like me as much as I like you. And don't girls like to be courted? And aren't guys supposed to distrust anything that comes too easy?

I'm already accepting the fact that you are not going to Santa Fe to have a picturesque place to send me emails and you want to see stuff, do stuff, and enjoy your friends. I hope you will and then tell me all about it.

Nancy Labastida

To: Charles Guittard

Thursday, September 9, 2021, at 6:25 a.m.

I woke up this morning and thought to myself, "I do need Charles. I don't know what I would do without him now." It really hit me, that now that you are in my life, I want you, and I need you, and I miss you all the time. I love you, yours, *Nancy*

Charles Guittard

To: Nancy Labastida

Thursday, September 9, 2021, at 3:00 p.m.

Emailed you early and often; talked to you by phone twice; took my meds; 20 laps at the J; picked up paw print & asked stranger a question at the vet; TC Jim; emailed with Helen and with Louise; forwarded their emails to NDL; texted Mary Hayes; ate lunch at Rockfish on Campbell Rd at Coit; tried to take an hour's nap but only stayed down 30 minutes; left voice mail message for Sid Files to call me; washed out Maggie's dog dish and little table and removed it from' entrance; couldn't find any tennis on T.V.; read the newspaper; thinking about cleaning up my apartment so the hoarding will be less obvious; ran a load of laundry; took a shower.

Charles Guittard

To: Nancy Labastida

Friday, September 10, 2021, at 1:10 p.m.

What to do this afternoon, work on my 2020 taxes or trade in the van. I'm choosing to trade in the van for a Toyota. More fun.

Charles Guittard

To: Nancy Labastida

Saturday, September 11, 2021, at 2:33 p.m.

[U.S. Open] Emma Raducanu is a -175 favorite (risk $175 to win $100) in the latest Leyla Fernandez vs. Raducanu odds from Caesars Sportsbook, with Fernandez getting +150 (risk $100 to win $140) as the underdog. Caesars set the over-under for total games at 21.5, with Raducanu favored by 2.5 games in the latest 2021 odds.

——————— ·•◦❧◦•· ———————

Nancy Labastida

To: Charles Guittard

Sunday, September 12, 2021, at 9:37 a.m.

Good morning, my dear Charles. First of all, I think it is a brilliant idea to give Katie a tennis racket and a can of balls for her birthday. Let's try to go to Irvine as soon as possible.

——————— ·•◦❧◦•· ———————

Charles Guittard

To: Nancy Labastida

Tuesday, September 14, 2021, at 1:05 a.m.

All of that below resonates with me, especially along the theme of "Is this really happening?" Add in for me "Is this a form of temporary insanity?" and "Could anyone like me as much as Nancy believes she does?" And then I think: "it is happening," "we are not beyond the pale of all reason," "we really do love each other," and "who deserves to be in love, and be loved at the age of 80, more than I do?" So it strongly appears that "we are good to go" and that it would be nuts and even sad to knock our thing to the ground.

———————⁕❈⁕———————

Charles Guittard

To: Nancy Labastida

Tuesday, September 14, 2021, at 7:31 a.m.

I am off to do my walk around the Pickens Hospice Lake.

Then for some oatmeal.

Then to talk again to Jim about our Irvine trip.

Then to a meeting of the council of our community.

Then for a haircut to delete weird hair.

Then to route some things to Georgette.

Then to order another tennis racket for Jim/Katia.

Then to Office Depot to replace some printer cartridges.

Then to other things, and from time to time checking my email.

Charles Guittard

To: Nancy Labastida

Tuesday, September 14, 2021, at 1:03 p.m.

I want you to see where I live too, although it will still look jammed-packed after I am somewhat able to de-clutter it. The good news is that it will <u>not</u> look like one of those places on "hoarders," one of those guilty pleasures like a food that would make you urp if you ate too much.

Charles Guittard

To: Nancy Labastida

Wednesday, September 15, 2021, at 10:22 a.m.

Cracked open my Goren book last night. I already remembered a lot but some stuff was totally new, like the rule on bidding major suits, like the five-card major rule and not bidding four-card majors, and other rules. Will dig in more tonight.

Charles Guittard

To: Nancy Labastida

Wednesday, September 15, 2021, at 6:02 p.m.

How about pork chops? I like all of those but we already had salmon. I love a sexy smart accomplished good-looking athletic woman who can also cook!

Charles Guittard

To: Nancy Labastida

Wednesday, September 15, 2021, at 6:15 p.m.

I don't think I have a favorite meal. Hmm, so what if I were on death row and entitled to ask for a last meal for the big house chef to cook? A last meal the chef would probably not know how to cook anyway? OK, I'll take a stab at it–swordfish, mushroom risotto, sauteed spinach, and a glass of wine. No need for appetizers, salad, dessert, or cappuccino.

Charles Guittard

To: Nancy Labastida

Thursday, September 16, 2021, at 3:26 p.m.

Half-packed up for tomorrow and have put together a little notebook of sample docs [Charles' book] for you. These are all before Georgette's edit but she probably won't change them much, at least not what they try to say.

It is a beautiful day in Dallas today. I met my new elderly next apartment neighbor pushing her walker slowly toward her door. She noticed the nameplate by my door and asked about Pat and told her Pat had passed in February; she said, "I'm sorry," and I said I was fine and had a girlfriend in Austin I was going to see.

Nancy Labastida

To: Charles Guittard

Monday, September 20, 2021, at 4:32 p.m.

That ("At Last") is the most beautiful and perfect song for us. It gave me shivers and made my eyes sting. All my love, *Nancy*

Charles Guittard

To: Nancy Labastida

Tuesday, September 21, 2021, at 6:10 p.m.

My dental appointment today was scheduled with a brand-new dental hygienist named Nicole Holstein. So young. But she was funny. I told her about my bad habit of eating ice. She laughed and said that meant my teeth were well-hydrated. I don't know how we got on the subject of "my girlfriend" since it would not necessarily come up in a dental appointment. She said she met her boyfriend named Rick online at a dating website called Bumble and that she liked the website because it only allowed women to initiate contact with men and not vice versa. Nicole took forever to clean my teeth. But she didn't blink when I told her I didn't want to hurt her feelings but I didn't need her to do the flossing as I am a maniac flosser myself. Then my dentist came in with a big smile on her face. I asked her if she had a new hairdo—for some reason that line always works with women—she gave me a big smile and said "yes." I was not in the "House of Pain" today. At least not for me!

Nancy Labastida

To: Charles Guittard

Thursday, September 23, 2021, at 5:04 p.m.

I am beginning to pack for my trip to Dallas.

My [bridge] friends all raved about you. You definitely meet with their approval. Rose couldn't be there because she was still recovering from Covid, but she said that on Monday, she woke up and felt 100% her old self.

I found the notes I wrote and the pictures I took of the day Alejandro [my 2d grandson] was born. That is what my book is about. I am so glad I wrote things down then. I remember almost every detail about the central story, but I had forgotten some things. I wish I had a few more pictures. I can hardly wait to read you what I have.

Charles Guittard

To: Nancy Labastida

Monday, September 27, 2021, at 8:19 a.m.

It's hard to believe my apartment is this tidy! Although you are not here with me which I was already regretting before you left, it is nice to be working in a slightly improved work area.

Charles Guittard

To: Nancy Labastida

Monday, September 27, 2021, at 12:15 p.m.

I'm going to wear these clunky orthopedic boots until it's time to go to Irvine. But who knows I may still be in the boots when we head to Irvine. Not a good look, sorry about that. Good luck with your rendezvous with the plumber.

Charles Guittard

To: Nancy Labastida

Monday, September 27, 2021, at 12:30 p.m.

Actually, the feet felt OK while you were in Dallas! But I want to give them a real rest, may have time for an appointment with Dr. Aston. Just finished up the rest of your seafood fettuccini from Lavendou. Really tasty and the aroma of garlic coming from the microwave was very nice.

Nancy Labastida

To: Charles Guittard

Monday, September 27, 2021, at 12:49 p.m.

Anyway, I hope the boys' bathroom can be fixed today. It's pretty major to fix mine. He did show me how to get cold water. I hope I can do it, when I take my next shower.

Charles Guittard

To: Nancy Labastida

Monday, September 27, 2021, at 1:08 p.m.

Georgette is working on the book. I am working on my taxes. You are working on those showers. Katie is starting to think about tennis. F [Fernando] and Y [Yami] are thinking about moving things along constructively.

Charles Guittard

To: Nancy Labastida

Monday, September 27, 2021, at 2:28 p.m.

Well, I was going to save all of this for later when we talked but I thought I would preserve it right now for "our posterity"! A lot of this just got rolled out because Sid's profession as a psychiatrist was asking personal questions to his patients and he is still very good at asking questions and getting answers.

So, my conversation with Sid went like this.

Hi, Sid, Nancy and I will be coming to Irvine and would like to drive to SD [San Diego] for a visit with you.

Sid: Have you and Nancy gotten married?

CG: No, we've only known each other for about a month.

Sid: Are you going to get married?

CG: (*pausing*) Probably.

Sid: Have you proposed to her yet?

CG: (*lots of hemming and hawing here*) Well, I'm not sure that I've made the classic proposal yet.

Sid: No problem. I can do it for you. I would love to... [*Sounds like he thinks he is Cyrano de Bergerac.*]

CG: No way, Sid, are you going to do it for me. You will remember that very inappropriate proposal you made to Pat to stay with you at your house and for me to go back to Dallas by myself. And you were married at the time.

Sid: Oh, yes. I'm very good at proposing. By the way, have you told her about all of your faults yet?

CG: That is hard to answer; one of my faults is I cannot easily identify my own faults.

Sid: Charles, you really have no faults. (Sid actually said this, but he is a great kidder.)

CG: Then why did you ask me that question?

Sid: I just like to ask questions.

CG: One of your faults is that you tend to exaggerate. *(and so on)*

Although I initially dodged Sid's question about whether I had made a formal proposal of marriage to you—after all, I have not told anyone else that I have proposed marriage or that I thought marriage was likely—I then more or less admitted it to Sid in the remarks which followed! He is just too good at asking questions and I am just too feeble in my attempts to dodge them and he is my oldest friend with all that experience at ferreting out answers to questions. And you know that at least as of this last weekend I have proposed!

Charles Guittard

To: Nancy Labastida

Tuesday, September 28, 2021, at 9:29 a.m.

My neighbor is hanging things again. Pound, pound, pound, pound, pound. Her bedroom wall adjoins my office. Now she is hanging things on other walls in her apartment. Sounds like she is settling in for the duration. I have another new neighbor across the hall; I haven't met her yet although I saw her relatives through a half-open door a week or so ago. The prior occupants of their apartment were interesting. One was a retired 94-year-old Navy lawyer named Ray. The other [next door] was an 80-year-old very heavy piano player named Carol.

Charles Guittard

To: Nancy Labastida

Tuesday, September 28, 2021, at 10:36 a.m.

I laughed when I saw that phrase "trial honeymoon." Such a funny idea. And no, it won't be quite living together, or we could just stitch together a series of "trial honeymoons." Living together will be much, much better I'm sure for me, anyway, since an ordinary, day-by-day life together with you is what inspires me much more than a series of passionate holidays. That movie I think starring Alan Alda in which he meets an old girlfriend at a hotel one day every year or every ten years is an entertaining idea for a movie but that's all; it doesn't get to where the rubber meets the road. So I started out laughing and then I got so serious!!!

Charles Guittard

To: Nancy Labastida

Tuesday, September 28, 2021, at 11:58 a.m.

This conversation is perhaps best left to pillow-talk but I'm sitting at my computer and you know what happens when I am sitting at my computer and you are on my mind. This morning I'm thinking about how the depth of my love for you has re-cast my loves for Lynn and Pat. Perhaps a strange subject, but a very real one for me, at least this morning before I've had my coffee. I truly loved Pat from several weeks after I met her, and there was a part of me that loved Lynn for a while [after our divorce]. But loving you has caused me to re-think those early loves, which perhaps I should not do. My love for Pat was a real one with lots of shared interests. I know I called Pat, before I met you, my life's vibrations, whatever that term means. And she was to the day she died.

But now there's Nancy and I just don't know how I can do you justice in words. You are just so wonderful and you are my life's vibrations and I don't know how I could have ever passed you up if I had ever been so lucky to meet you. So there are really no words at the present. Assuming for the moment that we get married down the road, that would certainly make a statement to the world of my affection for, you and commitment to you, but even changing our public relationship in that manner—which I long for—would only be a pale outline of the way I feel about you, dear Nancy. I am a loss for words; I suspect it will always be like that when I try to put my love in words for you. You remember the Mission Impossible Force's instruction—"Read this message; it will self-destruct in 60 seconds." However, you need not destroy this email but file it away with all the other messages about my affection for you.

Nancy Labastida

To: Charles Guittard

Tuesday, September 28, 2021, at 12:35 p.m.

I have been having the same kind of deep feelings about you and how different my love for you is from the love I felt for Fernando and also finding it hard to put into words. My love for you feels so new and wondrous. It has a lot to do with the exquisite way you treat me...I'm so comfortable with you, and I love talking to you and listening to you talk to me. I feel confident when I'm with you. I feel special all the time because of you. Your term "re-cast my love for...." makes all the sense in the world to me, because I have been doing the exact same thing, especially since our Dallas weekend. My eyes are stinging with tears as I type because of our magical relationship.

Charles Guittard

To: Nancy Labastida

Tuesday, September 28, 2021, at 7:30 p.m.

You have expressed a concern about all the money I've been spending lately related to you and me. Two things I need to say here. First, I have been on no fun outings anywhere with anyone since July 2013 because of Pat's health issues. Second, I have no objection to your spending money on things but it hasn't been important plus it really seemed to me that I should stand the expense of going to Irvine, etc. I've come to learn how sensitive and loving you are in these matters and I don't worry about that at all, as being generous is your basic nature. I don't believe in keeping an exact count of this sort of thing and I don't think couples should. There will always be nice things you can spend money on for you and me and I will just have to suck it up (LOL) and say, OK, dear, if you must. Perhaps I should also add that I am confident you will always be thinking of ways you can do your part, whatever that part is. I love you, Nancy, *Charles*

Charles Guittard

To: Nancy Labastida

Wednesday, September 29, 2021, at 10:07 a.m.

This morning I am wondering what it would have been like if I had met you in my last year at Baylor, perhaps at the Dallas Public Library when you worked there. The entire future of the world could have been different. LOL. If I had been mature enough to let you know who I am and vice versa, and you could have put up with someone who still had three more years of schooling to do.

Nancy Labastida

To: Charles Guittard

Wednesday, September 29, 2021, at 1:52 p.m.

Now I'm feeling sad that we did not meet in 1964 and that I did not help put you through law school, even if it was just being your adoring wife and making friends with other married students. We would have had a cute little apartment near the law school. You might have become a Democrat much earlier!!! I'm going to stop thinking about it and keep on thinking about the present and our future.

Nancy Labastida

To: Charles Guittard

Wednesday, September 29, 2021, at 2:26 p.m.

Charles, how nice and comfortable for you that you are making good progress and have kept all your information in good order. I admire that. I made an appointment for my booster [Covid]. It's for 9:30 tomorrow morning in Kyle! I'll be okay. I tried to make an appointment with a dermatologist, but the hold was so long that I gave up. I am going to try again, and this time, I will hold my place in line and have them call me back.

Belva and I came in last today. It was a shock, but I do know of 3 mistakes that I made. I bid 6NT and went down one. A crucial finesses didn't work. Three NT would have been a snap. Another time, I just bid 3 hearts, even though I had 8 hearts. With 8 in a suit, especially a major, I should go straight to game. I made 6. On that hand, both finesses worked!!! The one that hurt the most was an overcall of 2 hearts after they opened 1 spade. I expected them to go to 2 spades, but they passed. They both seemed to know that I could not make 2 hearts. I was down 3 vulnerable. It was painful.

Charles Guittard

To: Nancy Labastida

Wednesday, September 29, 2021, at 3:09 p.m.

Hindsight is 20-20. You are a splendid and fast bridge player and you take some chances. Sometimes that works and sometimes it doesn't. But that's what makes it fun. I liked watching you play my hands. Being slow, plodding, and ultra-conservative has to be boring. It seems to me it's not the contracts bid and made or the points gained, it's the excitement that comes from stretching a bit. I tend to be a boring player, but I want to take more chances. I will have to learn the bidding rules better first before I know enough to depart from them.

―――――――

Charles Guittard

To: Nancy Labastida

Wednesday, September 29, 2021, at 4:47 p.m.

As long as you are tight with your internist and your internist is not timid about making recommendations, you will make good decisions and you will be around for a long time yet and in good health and get to enjoy some great-grandchildren perhaps. Pat had an internist in Houston who was a little timid because of his cultural wiring to lean on her when he should have been more explicit. And then too Pat could have been more pro-active herself in her health matters.

I hope I'm not coming on too strong here since we are not married yet, but I will always wonder if I had been more involved with Pat's care earlier, whether her dementia could have been ameliorated somewhat. Probably not, but I will never know for sure and I did carry some guilt for a while. I just assumed for years that she was handling her health issues prudently and I told myself, that's her business, and she is a fully-competent adult. But married people, and couples like us, are a unit and what affects one person affects the other and both should be vitally interested in their partner's health. Hence, because I love you as my partner, I want to be allowed to speak to you about your health and your check-ups and to be informed to some extent, even if I may come across to you as being a nervous nellie. Because you are self-motivated mostly, I probably won't need to bug you, but I'm not going to take that off the table. And if I'm going to live with you, I'm probably the person who is going to know your health issues the best.

Nancy Labastida

To: Charles Guittard

Wednesday, September 29, 2021, at 5:15 p.m.

I do know that it can be dangerous for me to be too casual about my health and take it too much for granted, and that does worry me sometime, but not enough to be proactive. I don't have an internist. I go to the Austin Regional Clinic, and I have been happy with all the doctors I get, especially the one that took care of my hernia.

Fernando was too trusting of his homeopathic doctor, and I was alarmed and unhappy about it, but Fernando always studied books about health and homeopathy and made his own decisions. The kids and I virtually watched in stunned horror, as he kept searching for answers with alternative medicine. Young Fernando was on the verge of doing an intervention, when a Chinese acupuncturist told him [my husband Fernando] he needed to use traditional medicine. It was really too late. I always thought he knew what he was doing, and I didn't think I should or could stand up and be stronger in insisting that he give up his hopes for alternative medicine. So, Charles, we do need to watch out for each other. You can bug me. You are allowed to speak up about my health and check-ups. You can come to doctor visits with me. One thing is sure, I always have perfect blood pressure. There are almost no heart problems in my family.

I recognize that we will be taking care of each other, so we need to be involved with each other's health. I am not going to be stubborn or difficult; well, maybe just a little. I love you too much to be hurtful.

"THREE TO GET READY": THE PROPOSAL

Charles Guittard

To: Nancy Labastida

Thursday, September 30, 2021, at 9:18 a.m.

When I went to bed last night, I hadn't decided to propose this morning. But I did that expense thing, you liked it, and I went back to sleep. I woke up feeling very good about two hours later and sat down at my computer and thought, "Charles, old boy, why not go ahead and ask Nancy if she will marry you—she knows you're going to sooner or later anyway" and then I thought, "Sure, I will do that right now—I will call her up and tell her I have a question for her, then I will pause more than necessary for a second or two to add a little suspense to the moment, and then I will pop the question." "Charles, that is exactly what you should do," I told myself. And so I did and your answer was one word—"yes."

What are your thoughts about an exact day for our date with destiny?

John Guittard

To: Charles Francis Guittard

Thursday, September 30, 2021, at 10:44 a.m.

You guys work plenty max rapido! Max congratulations!

Nancy Labastida

To: Charles Guittard

Thursday, September 30, 2021, at 6:26 p.m,

Charles, I'm glad I told you it was okay to start telling people. You were bursting with the news. I had a hard time not talking about it at bridge today. Everybody was asking me how my weekend in Dallas was, though, so they know that we are definitely a couple. I can't think how to tell my children. I'd like to tell them together at a restaurant, but it's hard to get them together.

My arm is sore from my shot, and I'm feeling tired, but not sick or anything. Time for Wheel of Fortune!!! That's one thing you will learn about me!!!

Charles Guittard

To: Nancy Labastida

Friday, October 1, 2021, at 7:21 a.m.

My priorities are in order wedding planning, taxes, move to Austin, wedding, book. I note I have omitted honeymoon in there, presumably to follow the wedding. We haven't even talked about that. Gosh there is a lot to talk about, plan, and do right now! Maybe our honeymoon would include a trip to Houston to visit with Charlotte or with other friends in other places. Just brain-storming here. Or an Amtrak trip!!!

Charles Guittard

To: Nancy Labastida

Friday, October 1, 2021, at 7:49 a.m.

Maybe I could share that large bookcase with the late Fernando. Up to you of course.

Nancy Labastida

To: Charles Guittard

Friday, October 1, 2021, at 7:57 a.m.

I cannot think of a bookcase in this house that can be shared!!!! The large one is the most full. I guess I could remove some books to make room for yours. There are other book shelves that are not full of books, but have pictures and things on them along with books. Now that I am writing this, I am sure I can remove a lot of the books in the front room to make space for your books.

Charles Guittard

To: Nancy Labastida

Friday, October 1, 2021, at 1:12 p.m.

See what you think of this [Charles' handout for the Davis emergency Zoom meeting]. I tried hard to reduce it to one page. I hope it is helpful; it is bound to fill in some gaps.

Charles' Info

School: grade school UP; HPJHS 1yr: Hillcrest HS 5 years 55-60; 5-yr band letter; debater 2 years; played sousaphone and then trombone.

College: Baylor in Waco, English & Philosophy, Theology minor; debate team.

Law school: SMU; coached 1st year moot court teams to 1st place finishes.

Law practice: settled into business litigation and did that for many years; changed direction in 1994, diving into mediation, and was a leader in the ADR movement in Texas. Founded the Dallas Bar's Business Litigation Section; later chaired the State Bar's Alternative Dispute Resolution Section; elected to the Dallas Bar's Board of Directors.

Pro bono or substantially pro bono: Taught negotiation as an adjunct at SMU and University of Houston; coached winning teams at SMU and South Texas College of Law. My mediation practice and teaching and coaching law students were the most satisfying parts of my legal career.

Scholarships: Endowed scholarships at Baylor and Centenary (Pat's and Steve Moffatt's alma mater). Facilitated the creation of the history Ph.D. program and Baylor and the Guittard Book Award in History.

Retirement: Working on the last volume of a trilogy entitled *I WILL TEACH HISTORY* about my grandfather Frank Guittard and his life & times.

Marriage no 1: to Lynn Bussey of Dallas, producing two sons, Jim and Bob; ending in divorce after 11 years. Jim is a chaplain for Vitas Hospice in Irvine; Bob is a development VP for UT in Austin; 4 grandchildren: Miles, Charlie, Finn, and Katie, oldest is 13, youngest 6.

Marriage no 2: to Pat (Verlander) Moffatt of Hammond LA; very happy 35 years, successful blended family; took trips to the Amazon, South America, Manhattan, England, Israel, Austria, Hungary, and Australia/NZ among other places, sometimes to sing with choruses Pat was a member of; stepson Steve Moffatt, same age as Jim Guittard.

Hobbies: emailing; reading, movies, opera, travel, restaurants, etc.; mediocre club tennis player in the late 50s—can no longer play; Harvey Davis Jr. hammered me the one time we played; passionate bridge player in the late 50s and the 60s and relearning the bidding rules so I can play with Nancy; hopeless at golf—could not master the grip or the swing.

Parents: Father Clarence retired as Chief Justice of the Dallas Court of Appeals. Mother was a wife and mother of two boys and one girl, and was active in many Dallas clubs.

What I love about Nancy: Funny, affectionate, sympathetic, honest, agreeable, easy to talk to, collaborative, loves opera and music, has her own interests, independent, beloved by her family, bright, energetic, unselfish, supportive, patient, loyal, centered and stable.

Charles Guittard

To: Steve Moffatt, Bob Guittard, Jim Guittard

Bcc: Nancy Labastida

Friday, October 1, 2021, at 4:02 p.m.

The Davises are having an emergency zoom meeting tonight to address the news that Nancy and I are planning to get married. Since my future is going to be discussed and there has been little or no time for them to get to know me, I decided to prepare the attached [handout]. I'm told most of the Davises have already decided I'm a fairly good guy. So I hope the result of the meeting will be positive and returned quickly.

———————————

Guittard, Bob

To: Charles Guittard

Friday, October 1, 2021, at 4:12 p.m.

I wouldn't leave out that you like to travel, love humor in all forms, love movies and reading, and have a faith that's important to you. and that you're always curious, interested in many things and learning, and you don't tend to slip into the lazy, do nothing but watch TV, and have someone take care of you and bring you meals mode. You're a great and caring spouse, who very much encourages and supports the interests and passions and hobbies of your wife. My mom has talked about how you did this for her, and I know did for Pat. Steve also lived with you for more years than I did and could be asked about your day to day year in and year out temperament at home and how you lovingly treated his mom for those years, as well cared for her so well and so selflessly in the hard recent years.

Charles Guittard

To: Bob Guittard

Friday, October 1, 2021, at 4:21 p.m.

Gosh, Bob, I don't know what to say except thanks. I've already sent the original version to Nancy to use as she wishes but will pass your kind remarks also on to her. It's little like one of those game shows where a contestant has one or two life-lines they can call if they need to.

Charles Guittard

To: Nancy Labastida

Friday, October 1, 2021, at 5:18 p.m.

Please don't ask Talbot even out of an abundance of caution about his credentials to marry people. I would look like an idiot which I probably am.

Charles Guittard

To: Nancy Labastida

Friday, October 1, 2021, at 7:10 p.m.

Talked to Bob who will bring his guitar and back up Bill who will have to do the singing. Bob seemed to think the prospect of backing Bill up was an exciting one and he's ready to go with no preparation whatsoever. He also has an extra guitar or two for Jim to use as well. So I think we just throw these guys together and see what happens like a chemistry experiment.

Nancy Labastida

To: Charles Guittard

Saturday, Oct 2, 2021, at 8:32 a.m.

Charles, I think that it is perfect that you release your room as of November 30. Do it!!! In the meantime, when you come to Austin, I would like you to bring the books and the pictures that you want to have in this house, so that we can make it more "our house." You can bring a load each trip.

———————————— ·:•◦❧◦•:· ————————————

Charles Guittard

To: Nancy Labastida

Saturday, October 2, 2021, at 8:46 a.m.

OK will do. I'll bring some books and some pictures and take a look at the space you can make available. Sometimes for me less is more—it is a good discipline I need to practice more often—and I can whittle mine down while figuring out which books and research files to keep in storage in Dallas. I admit I like the phrase "more like our house." However, it does not bother me that it will forever be "Nancy's house" and that I am a special occupant, namely, your "hubbie."

Nancy Labastida

To: Charles Guittard

Saturday, October 2, 2021, at 9:21 a.m.

Well, yes, it is my house in the sense that it is in my estate, but it's our house in the sense that you will be living here, too. You need to see familiar things of yours in the house, and I need to remove things that are no longer right to have around. Believe me, if I were moving into your house, I would not want constant reminders of Pat. I would hate that. You can be assured that just about everything in our house was chosen by me. It reflects my taste. I'm so glad I completely changed up my bedroom just before and during covid. You will not be a visitor in my house, and I want you to feel comfortable and at home. Fernando told me that your computer can easily be installed anywhere in the house. Maybe I can get Alejandro to come over when you are here to help rearrange the furniture in the front room.

Charles Guittard

To: Nancy Labastida

Saturday, October 2, 2021, at 9:41 a.m.

When you said you would not want to see constant reminders of Pat if you were in my house (which I don't have anymore), I had to smile, as I feel somewhat the same way about the late Fernando with at least one important qualification—your house should always feel very welcoming to your children and grandchildren and all of those family pictures and Fernando pictures are an important part of their family legacy and history; they do not need to be thinned out or go to storage. Your family would be very upset if anyone messed with those family pictures and the new guy would catch billy heck. I do welcome Fernando and Alejandro's input and help into getting me set up. I'm sure Bob would appear at a moment's notice if additional help was needed. *Your first Charles*

Nancy Labastida

To: Charles Guittard

Saturday, October 2, 2021, at 9:53 a.m.

I think some of the things were probably more important to me than to the children and grandchildren. I don't think anyone would be upset if I messed with the family pictures. I'll be thinking about it all in the next days. I'm thinking more about the ones in the front room that can be moved. Things will happen gradually. I do think that even my children and grandchildren would feel uncomfortable with Fernando pictures all around after you move in. It will be a process.

I called my beloved grandson [Fernando Xavier] in Philadelphia just a few minutes ago. He had told his father [Fernando Augusto] that he is worried that it might be too soon and hoping that I'm not rushing into things. This morning he told me that he loves me very much, and he only wants my happiness. I'm hoping that he can come to the wedding.

Charles Guittard

To: Mary Hayes

Bcc: Nancy Labastida

Saturday, October 2, 2021, at 10:01 a.m.

Mary, I'm afraid you're going to be stunned, so you may need to sit down. Nancy and I are going to be married December 11 in Austin. Her brother called an emergency zoom meeting with her other brothers and sisters (there are six of them)—some of them possibly alarmed by the news of our connection—and I was hashed and re-hashed, although I wasn't present to defend myself. However, apparently, I passed the inspection even though one of Nancy's brothers (a lawyer) at the end still wanted me to submit five references, supposedly a joke. Nancy and I have learned more about each other in less than two months than most people could learn in years of casual dating or perhaps a lifetime. Your friend who is still in debt to you for all you did for dear Pat.

"AND FOUR TO GO!": FROM RING TO CEREMONY

Nancy Labastida

To: Charles Guittard

Saturday, October 2, 2021, at 4:18 p.m.

Charles, I went window shopping for a wedding ring today. I'm trying to get ideas.

———— ·•◦❧◦•· ————

Charles Guittard

To: Nancy Labastida

Saturday, October 2, 2021, at 4:50 p.m.

It makes me feel very good that you are looking for a ring, especially since you've not had one previously, and I'm the guy that gets the thrill of doing that for you. I've about come up with a ring budget, but if you wanted to add something to it, it wouldn't hurt my feelings at all.

Nancy Labastida

To: Virginia Palmer, Bill Oliver, Harvey Davis, A. Gayle Hudgens, Charlotte Seifert, and 12 more...

Sunday, October 3, 2021, at 8:39 a.m.

I am copying the email that Charles sent out to his family almost word for word. Please save the date! Invitations will be mailed. The marriage will take place as follows:

Date: Saturday, December 11, 2021

Place: Nancy's house, Austin, Texas

Time: 5:00 pm

Dress: Casual

Food: To follow the ceremony, probably barbecue or Mexican

Music: To follow the ceremony: some jamming, some singing. It's going to be fairly wild. There will be acoustic guitars and who knows what. Maybe a harmonica, if anyone knows how to play one.

Covid requirements: Vaccinations, not masks are essential. The vaccination condition is because of a number of factors: 1. Charles and Nancy and most attendees are seniors. 2. There will be persons present with underlying health conditions. 3. There will be children present. 4. The event will take place entirely in Nancy's house. 5. Nancy and Charles don't want this to be on the 10:00 news for spreading the virus with the headline: "Seniors' caution-less nuptials spread the virus in loony late-life ceremony."

We look forward to seeing everyone. It will be an event to remember.

Charles Guittard

To: Jim Guittard, Katia Guittard

Sunday, October 3, 2021, at 4:34 p.m.

I know you both must have a strong conviction about Covid vaccinations or you would already be vaccinated. I admire strong convictions and the way you have lived your lives. I would hope that where the wedding is concerned, without abandoning your convictions generally, you might make an exception for me and Nancy so you can be with us on our special day. Nancy was, as was I, distressed to hear that the three of you would not be with me or us on December 11. Sometimes our principles are in conflict and choices must be made. And sometimes too exceptions can be justified because of special circumstances without abandoning one's principles. Nancy and I are hoping that you can see your way clear to making an exception for us.

If you, K and K are unable to come, it will not affect our relationship but we will really miss you and feel that some important part of our day—a once in a lifetime kind of thing—was missing. Love to you, K and K.

[*Author's note: Jim and Katia, based on their conscientious objection to COVID-19 inoculations, decided not to attend the wedding.*]

Charles Guittard

To: Nancy Labastida

Sunday, October 3, 2021, at 6:00 p.m.

One of the reasons I thought it was kind of funny you provided your phone number several times to me in your emails was that in the letters from Josie Glenn to Frank Guittard in which he was passionately pursuing her, she mentioned her phone number two or three times, it was "Hadley..." Just a little bit of Guittard trivia.

Nancy Labastida

To: Charles Guittard

Sunday, October 3, 2021, at 6:07 p.m.

What a fun coincidence about the courtship of Frank and Josie and Charles and Nancy! *Your devoted fiancée, Nancy*

Charles Guittard

To: Nancy Labastida

Sunday, October 3, 2021, at 6:27 p.m.

Yes, indeed, and he was even bolder than I have been and was almost from the beginning exuding this "it's going to happen—you might as well give into it—it's bigger than both of us Uncle Miltie" kind of vibe where Josie was concerned. I've always been, at least closer to the outset, "Well, Nancy dear, I hope in time you will like me as much as I like you, etc., etc." —rather mild by comparison, don't you think? Frank was a man on a mission with a four-year-old son who needed a mother and was living in Shiner with relatives. And Frank had been without a wife for three-plus years following Mamie's death at the sanatorium.

Actually, on mature reflection, I have fairly determined, at least as of the time that we shared the "L" word, I stood up increasingly for what I wanted well enough, but then "faint heart ne'er won fair lady." One source I've found for that aphorism, supposedly a Middle English saying, round about 1545 A.D.: *"A coward verely neuer obteyned the loue of a faire lady."* *[1545 R. Taverner tr. Erasmus' Adages (ed. 2) 10]*

Nancy Labastida

To: Charles Guittard

Tuesday, October 5, 2021, at 6:23 a.m.

You might be surprised to know that the need to be reassured pops up in my feelings from time to time during any given day, too. Sometimes, when I write a particularly loving email, I think, "Oh, he might think I'm too crazy about him and the hunt is over and I'm too easy and he is bored and wants to hunt again for the thrill of conquering another heart." Then I tell myself that that's wrong and I need to feel confident in your love. Almost every minute of every day, I feel loved and cherished. I am overcome with feeling of love for you many times a day.

Your words and thoughts of you are in my head every waking moment. Even when I am talking to another person, you are always in my head and in my heart, and I feel special even when I am acting normal. I love you my darling Charles, *Nancy*

Charles Guittard

To: Nancy Labastida

Tuesday, October 5, 2021, at 6:55 a.m.

Be completely reassured. You are not crazy. You are not easy. I am not bored. My very short "hunt" —if it was that, is over. I could never imagine "capturing" another heart could compare to what has happened between us.

Nancy Labastida

To: Charles Guittard

Tuesday, October 5, 2021, at 2:52 p.m.

Haha. After complaining about my points, I opened 1 club with a good club suit and 11 points. Abby bid 6 clubs, and I made 7 clubs. She had 21 points.

Charles Guittard

To: Nancy Labastida

Tuesday, October 5, 2021, at 7:52 p.m.

What I seem to be learning every day is that it would be impossible for me to be partners with you and live apart from you and still be productive. Living in Dallas I am able to do basic things like going to the grocery, medical appointments, let phlebotomists draw blood, show friendliness to random strangers, pick up the mail, do little routine mindless things, pay a bill or two, brush my teeth, take my meds, but my real productive energy all goes into emails, texts, poem revisions, buying you socks, thinking about living with you, and just dreaming about you. I seem to have years of unexpressed and undirected passion and love wanting to come out and now coming out at last and it's all focused on you, the wonderful person who has, whether she knew it or not, tapped that reservoir.

So I will now start back on my taxes with that bit of emotion discharged from a fairly bottomless well, calm myself back down, try to let discipline and reason take charge, and think about deductions, income, etc., etc. as best I can until you call me with the results of the tournament. *Charles*

Nancy Labastida

To: Charles Guittard

Tuesday, October 5, 2021, at 9:21 p.m.

In your amazing, beautiful way, you have made me realize that I feel the same way about you, especially what you say about years of unexpressed love and undirected passion just yearning to come out. I am almost afraid to say it, but I have never loved so deeply or been loved so deeply. It's wondrous, and it's all I have ever wanted. I knew somewhere deep down that I was always missing something, and now I have found it in you. It is the most delicious feeling imaginable to feel this depth and joy of loving utterly and knowing that I am equally loved. I don't want to sound too crazy, but I hope we die together. I should never say that, but I know you understand me. I want to hold your hand and die happy with you one day in the far future.

I was going to call you, but you can call me when you read this. By the way, we came in 6th out of 28 couples and 3rd N/S. *Nancy*

Charles Guittard

To: Nancy Labastida

Wednesday, October 6, 2021, at 7:04 a.m.

We not only have a story, we have a book to write after we finish writing our other books. It will require an introduction and then some judicious editing. It will also require some sensitivity to the feelings of our children, probably your children more than mine, but our late-life romance of lovers who unknowingly went through their early years together yet apart and finally connected after so many years and after the spouses of both had passed away, is a fine story to tell and leave as a legacy. How about this for a title? "At Last! The Story of Charles and Nancy Who Finally Found Each Other told in 1000 emails."

Charles Guittard

To: Nancy Labastida

Wednesday, October 6, 2021, at 8:45 a.m.

And before we started talking, I thought my future was limited to a rare visit with my rambunctious grandchildren, a hard lonely grind finishing my book, and possibly occasional coffee dates with miscellaneous emotionally unavailable old prunes. Whew! I've dodged a bullet!

Nancy Labastida

To: Charles Guittard

Wednesday, October 6, 2021, at 9:25 a.m.

Or you could come down on Thursday. I play bridge from 1:00 until about 4:00. Maybe that's crazy. Just something to think about.

Charles Guittard

To: Nancy Labastida

Wednesday, October 6, 2021, at 9:25 a.m.

They are really old here at The Reserve—average age high 80s—and they creep around pushing their walkers and talk about the food they like and don't like and gather in little cluster-gab sessions waiting for the mailman. Yikes!

Nancy Labastida

To: Charles Guittard

Wednesday, October 6, 2021, at 9:27 a.m.

Oh, Charles! Get the hell out of there as quickly as possible. You need fresh air and me.

Nancy Labastida

To: Charles Guittard

Wednesday, October 6, 2021, at 10:12 a.m.

I'm getting my nails done now, so my hands will look good for the ring. Appointment at 3.

Charles Guittard

To: Nancy Labastida

Wednesday, October 13, 2021, at 9:14 a.m.

[Regarding Nancy's former brother-in-law] Maybe Jorge [Labastida] doesn't want Rosaelena to marry again if he goes first? Just a thought.

Nancy Labastida

To: Charles Guittard

Wednesday, October 13, 2021, at 3:15 p.m.

Hahaha! I'm sure he will not want Rosaelena to marry again if he goes first. He would hate that more than you can imagine, especially since she is going to be a very rich widow. I think Jorge just hates the thought that I would ever love another man.

Charles Guittard

To: Nancy Labastida

Wednesday, October 13, 2021, at 4:01 p.m.

I think if that if Jorge is really against our marriage, I think we should tie him up and make him eat tripe. Or if he likes tripe, then rocky mountain oysters, or if he likes them too, then I don't know what.

Charles Guittard

To: Nancy Labastida

October 17, 2021, 7:30 a.m.

I sincerely hope Brian [jeweler] is at work on your ring. As Dr. Bruce Banner would turn into the Hulk when he became angry, Brian would not want to see me all angry and humongous and green like the Hulk. And you can quote me. Currently not angry, humongous or green.

Charles Guittard

To: Nancy Labastida

Sunday, October 17, 2021, at 8:09 a.m.

I looked at a map. Here is one idea for a honeymoon:

December 11 Austin at the Four Seasons

December 12 drive to Houston to visit with Charlotte and stay at a Houston hotel

December 13 drive to Galveston, do Pleasure Pier and stay at a Galveston hotel

December 14 return to Houston perhaps via a night in San Antonio if we have time

Whaddyyathink? Suggest any variations of the above you like.

Nancy Labastida

To: Charles Guittard

Sunday, October 17, 2021, at 9:14 a.m.

Charles, I hope you never become angry and humongous and green. I certainly don't want to see that!!!

Nancy Labastida

To: Charles Guittard

Monday, October 18, 2021, at 6:05 a.m.

I will probably tell them [Nancy's Mexican former in-laws] in English, since all of them except for Jorge speak English, and Jorge already knows [we are going to be married]. I won't be nervous! Hahaha. I like that Charles has been chasing me for two months, and we both need some sleep. I will also use the toy boy angle. It will be fun. I'll see if someone can video me. I'll say how Clayton wanted 5 references and how Talbot asked if you know how old I am. You are so funny. I know some of those women at the Reserve have been eyeing you. Must go have my Cheerios now.

Charles Guittard

To: Nancy Labastida

Monday, October 18, 2021, at 9:46 a.m.

I've had so little experience in proposing I'm sure I would have been totally bummed out if you had said "no." The women on walkers would have moved in and finished me off.

Charles Guittard

To: Nancy Labastida

Tuesday, October 19, 2021, at 7:37 p.m.

Somehow I'm getting more of these solicitations to try out for legal jobs. Must be a sign the economy has some life left in it. They apparently don't know that I'm an octogenarian engaged to an octogenarian and haven't looked at a law book in almost 3 decades. Of those mentioned, director of career services would be the most congenial to my personality. Driven is the company that furnishes wheelchairs and that sounds kind of lame, doesn't it? I would be hiring attorneys to defend cases by people who were ejected by their wheelchairs or fell out of their wheelchairs or crashed into other people in wheelchairs, or run over by people in nursing homes on those little scooter things! Give me a break! I'm retired; I just want to read, play bridge, watch T.V., go to Waterloo, and let my girlfriend feed me bonbons. And finish my book to get Mary Hayes off my back.

Nancy Labastida

To: Charles Guittard

Monday, October 25, 2021, at 7:27 a.m.

I got a summons for jury duty a couple of weeks ago, and I put it aside to answer later, and then forgot about it. I found it just now, and the deadline to answer is tomorrow. I have just now answered it and got my exemption for being over 70. Whew, they could have wanted me for Dec. 11!

Charles Guittard

To: Nancy Labastida

Tuesday, October 26, 2021, at 8:37 a.m.

[As to choice of music for the wedding ceremony] I guess "A Hunka, Hunka of Burning Love" might be too suggestive.

Nancy Labastida

To: Charles Guittard

Tuesday, October 26, 2021, at 9:00 a.m.

Hahaha, no we cannot have that, nor can we have the uncomfortable suggestion that we might have sex.

Charles Guittard

To: Nancy Labastida

Tuesday, October 26, 2021, at 9:05 a.m.

Seniors do not have sex. It is unseemly and embarrasses the younger set.

Charles Guittard

To: Nancy Labastida

Tuesday, October 26, 2021, at 9:30 a.m.

The new maintenance lady is cleaning my apartment and washing the sheets!! First time ever. Maybe a special perk for those who are moving out. Or part of a fumigation protocol.

Charles Guittard

To: Nancy Labastida

Wednesday, October 27, 2021, at 6:00 a.m.

I'm up but probably not for the day. Just couldn't sleep anymore as I am thinking about all the things I need to move, store, pack up, toss, donate, etc. It is lightly raining. The contacts and photos which were to have been moved to my new phone have not transferred yet. Boo, hoo, hoo.

Georgette is almost through with her "first pass" edit of the manuscript which was 90 percent of the total work, leaving only two chapters to finalize and send her. Since my off-task time courting you has delayed—in a very wonderful way to be sure—my work on the book, and I'm sure she would like to be paid something for her work to date which I've yet to inspect, I'm going to send her another partial payment so that she will be paid 60 percent as of today. She has been very nice to work with to this point.

I'm going to tap "send" when it is 6:00 a.m. on the dot and then go have a little breakfast. I gained three pounds during your trip to Dallas even though you did not cook anything—go figure! I love you Nancy. It's 6:00. *Charles at apartment 1119*

Charles Guittard

To: Nancy Labastida

Wednesday, October 27, 2021, at 8:59 a.m.

I am always interested in dreams and would love to hear yours. I assume they wouldn't be too scary for me to hear. When I was a freshman or sophomore at Baylor, I bought a copy of Freud's book on the interpretation of dreams. I started summarizing all of my dreams in a little notebook until I had over 60 dreams. It was amazing how many things in my dreams were symbols for sexual things and also how many other things were just weird. I didn't try to interpret them, just get them down in my little notebook. I hope I lost that notebook. LOL.

Charles Guittard

To: Nancy Labastida

Wednesday, November 3, 2021, at 5:45 p.m.

Since I was not planning to bring my chest of drawers with me, do you suggest after I move in getting something handy from the Container Store that I can just keep in that closet for my underwear, tee shirts, socks, sweats, etc.?

Nancy Labastida

To: Charles Guittard

Wednesday, November 3, 2021, at 5:50 p.m.

Charles, I'm emptying a chest in the bedroom for you. Don't worry about where your things will go. There's room.

Charles Guittard

To: Nancy Labastida

Friday, November 5, 2021, at 8:49 a.m.

So sorry you have the same cold I am getting rid of. It looks like you may have gotten it from me. I have not had a cold in maybe five years and now it seems I have given it to the last person I would want to give it to. There is a Spike Jones song but I won't quote it because I know you are hurting. Here is what I have been taking:

1 Zinc cold therapy (quick dissolving tablets, citrus flavor) to reduce symptoms (Walgreen's)

2 Chloraseptic sore throat spray (CVS or Walgreen's)

3 Walgreen's Nighttime Multi-symptom Cold & Flu; compares to Vick's Nyquil ingredients

The first is a tablet that reduces symptoms if taken at the outset of a cold, the second a spray that knocks out sore throat, and the third a syrupy medication that calms the coughing. They all do multiple things that make things better. Hopefully, Rosaelena can quickly get you some medicine where you will feel well enough for the concert tomorrow night. It took me three days to feel better and you will feel better too in a few.

Charles Guittard

To: Nancy Labastida

Saturday, November 6, 2021, at 8:22 a.m.

I had a great night's sleep last night. Hope you are OK this a.m. I miss our pillow-talk and book-reading. That was really special when I read you "The Tell-Tale Heart"; you were hanging on every word so quietly I thought you were asleep and yet you seemed electrified when I read the last few words, "the beating of his hideous heart." Your eyes were so big—half startled, half-amused, but completely captured by Mr. Poe's poem! *Your lover boy, Charles*

Nancy Labastida

To: Charles Guittard

Saturday, November 6, 2021, at 10:01 a.m.

I told Rosaelena that I'm not sure if I'm well, so Jorge is going to have his moment of glory—analyzing my symptoms. He cut a tiny lock of hair from the back of my head. I hope you won't miss it! Haha. Now, he is putting it in his machine. I'm waiting with baited breath.

Charles Guittard

To: Nancy Labastida

Saturday, November 6, 2021, at 10:12 a.m.

Never heard of such a thing! Sounds pretty nutty. With Jorge you not only get a lawyer you get a doctor too!

Nancy Labastida

To: Charles Guittard

Saturday, November 6, 2021, at 10:16 a.m.

You nailed it, Charles! Rosaelena has nothing to do with the machine. He spends hours at it. It's like "the other woman." He claims to be able to cure people. We will see. He's been at the machine for a long time now.

Nancy Labastida

To: Charles Guittard

Saturday, November 6, 2021, at 10:30 a.m.

Jorge says my larynx is irritated because of some metals in the air. He wanted to give me some homeopathic pills but couldn't because I drank coffee too recently. He put a patch on my arm. Jorge is still in pajamas, and Rose is getting a manicure. I ate a delicious banana bar that Rose made without sugar or flour. I'll be fine. At least Jorge didn't say I have flu. I've been masking. You are mine at last, *Nancy.*

Charles Guittard

To: Nancy Labastida

Saturday, November 6, 2021, at 10:59 a.m.

"Your larynx is irritated because of metals in the air?" How weird is that? There seems to be a definite weirdness that tends to run in the male Labastida lawyers who think they are also doctors! Don't take any homeopathic pills from a lawyer who thinks he is also a doctor. I wouldn't wear that patch–probably harmless but who knows what the hell it is doing? I'm getting worried now. I may have to email Fernando Augusto to rescue you from Jorge's "care." Do you have access to a real doctor? Please get Rosaelena to find you one. This is starting to get very aggravating. You are so willing to please everyone, even to the extent of taking nutty homeopathic cures you know are nutty and without value. I'm going to put Fernando Augusto on speed-dial.

Nancy Labastida

To: Charles Guittard

Saturday, November 6, 2021, at 11:11 a.m.

Nooooooo! No rescuing by Fernando Augusto. I have indulged the Labastida family's passion for homeopathic medicine for 58 years, and I'm not going to stop now. Actually, there are certain medicines that have helped me. Maybe my translation was lacking maybe it's more like polluted air has affected my larynx. Don't worry. Homeopathy is harmless. If it works, great, if not, no harm done. I'll be home soon, and all will be right with the world.

Charles Guittard

To: Nancy Labastida

Saturday, November 6, 2021, at 11:23 a.m.

OK, I won't call Fernando yet. Seriously, I have books talking about all the cockamamie machines that have competed with true medicine and doctors for decades and decades. Usually harmless except when they distract patients from finding real medical care and wasted valuable time that could have been put to better use by finding real medical care. This is almost sounding like an argument. You know that I love you and don't want you to take any chances with your health.

Charles Guittard

To: Nancy Labastida

Saturday, November 6, 2021, at 9:20 p.m.

I have really made a lot of progress with the book and now am looking at the light at the end of the tunnel. I will be through the tunnel in another day or two, maybe by tomorrow. Then I switch to clothes. I'm thinking I will pick up a couple of the large bags I have in storage and fold up a lot of the clothes for those bags. Some of my clothes that are in good condition I've never worn because I don't much care for them and I will take those to Goodwill. I can't tell that any of my books have been taken [from the piles in the hall] although if a few were taken, I would not be able to tell. I don't have any bestsellers if that is the type of book those people were looking for. *Charles after a full day*

Nancy Labastida

To: Charles Guittard

Monday, November 8, 2021, at 8:53 a.m.

Great. I couldn't make reservations online for a party of two for either Saturday or Sunday, and it would have to be at 9:00 on Friday, so I picked Monday, really pricey, and I'll use our joint account. We'll celebrate our joint account day! If it's Fonda San Miguel, it's a big treat for me. I haven't been there in years.

Charles Guittard

To: Nancy Labastida

Monday, November 8, 2021, at 8:58 a.m.

Sounds like a great place to celebrate JAD (Joint Account Day)! Should I wear my best sweat suit or my only pair of jeans?

Nancy Labastida

To: Charles Guittard

Tuesday, November 9, 2021. at 6:57 a.m.

Yikes! We need to discuss about Christmas and the invitation for Christmas Eve. We are going to have our first lesson in belonging to new families!!! I just sent a nice email to Louise Kee, telling her that we would discuss the invitation and answer soon. I'm so glad to be back, and I had a very good night's sleep. Now, I'm changing the clocks in the house and thinking about my day and the future.

Charles Guittard

To: Nancy Labastida

Tuesday, November 9, 2021, at 8:25 a.m.

So we will have to map out how we deal with Christmas and Thanksgiving gatherings and assorted birthday gatherings. I am now, or shortly will be, part of a new family or families in Austin while still being a member of Dallas families. The same for you but being the reverse. I will make a list of the expected gatherings in

Dallas and Austin along with who might be normally expected to attend. I'm not sure what family gatherings the Davises and Labastidas do in Austin. You will have to let me know.

I think the place to start is for you to confer with both Candace and with Jo and Louise at some point. I haven't brought up the topic of gift-giving and that could be very complicated or very simple. Since you and I will be married, some of our little gifts might be from both of us, and not just me or you. I think we can work this out without hiring the Thrash firm. LOL. So what are your thoughts? My hunch is with our marriage and with Bob and Candace now being in Austin, there is a whole new era in the making.

Charles Guittard

To: Nancy Labastida

Wednesday, November 10, 2021, at 8:10 p.m.

It seems like things continue to happen at apartment 1119 in regard to kitchen stuff, books, things to Goodwill, and things to The Reserve's garage Sale, which occurs next week and I just found out about today. I have picked out some books to bring with me to Austin that I hope will provide entertaining bedtime reading to be read aloud—fairy tales, Lamb's tales from Shakespeare, famous myths, books of poetry, and some other books containing short pieces. I can't find the ghost story books I used to have, darn it. I love to read to you and to be read to.

Charles Guittard

To: Nancy Labastida

Thursday, November 11, 2021, at 7:15 a.m.

I could not sleep or didn't want to any longer after waking up to my phone with its Amber alert feature which coincided handily with an early nature call.

Pretty easy to do what I have to do today—just mess with a bunch of boxes, pack the car, and call Cody at Fidelity. I think I'll put off getting my haircut until next week which will leave about three weeks until the big day. Any bad haircut will have a chance to even out a bit and not look so obviously just cut. I may even get back into the kitchen and throw away some more stuff in the pantry. Basically, I'm just tossing everything in the pantry—sticky syrup bottles, boxes of cereal, sacks of coffee, the coffee machine, old grocery plastic sacks, and there are a lot of them, everything.

Nancy Labastida

To: Charles Guittard

Wednesday, November 17, 2021, at 5:51 a.m.

Good morning, my beloved Charles. I cannot imagine life without you now. I have never had so much fun or laughed so much or loved so much as I do now with you. Decisions are so easy with you. Life is fun and joyous with you. I love you with all my heart, and I can hardly wait to become your wife

Charles Guittard

To: Nancy Labastida

Tuesday, November 23, 2021, at 10:01 a.m.

I gave them [Junk Haulers] a good tip—will be the best they'll receive all day. I don't know what came over me, just in a good mood, a Christmas kind of mood, kind of like Uncle Scrooge on Christmas morning. I also talked cap pistols and whips with Darrell the lead mover and pulled out that cap pistol I bought on Ebay. Out in the hall an elderly lady (say 90) in a wheelchair was going through my books and I explained to her why there were so many. I gave her some of the best cookbooks—she has a collection. She is a retired investigator for the Texas Employment Commission. She also told me she always wanted to learn how to play piano and I just happened to have an instructional book & DVD and gave it to her. I asked her if she had a keyboard and she said "No, but I can get one."

Mary Hayes' "husband" Broderick Mosley is coming tomorrow for the wardrobe and the bed. That's making me a little nervous. Anyway, all is well (until it isn't well, LOL).

Nancy Labastida

To: Charles Guittard

Tuesday, November 23, 2021, at 11:44 a.m.

Okay, Charles. That's fine. Tomorrow is a busy day here. Joel is going to start the demolition of the bathroom. Fernando can show you how to use the other shower. Telma (the cleaning lady) will be here. I hope by the time you get here, things will be calming down. We'll enjoy a little dinner and a little wine.

Nancy Labastida

To: Charles Guittard

Sunday, November 28, 2021, at 4:34 p.m.

I think you are nearing the end of your massive job of clearing out your stuff and leaving the Reserve and moving to Austin. I went to Goodwill today and dropped off the box of glasses that we don't need and all the clothes that were thrown on the floor of the closet in the office. I have also emptied one drawer in the desk. I think I will empty the other tomorrow.

Soon, my love, we'll be together forever. *Your Nancy*

Charles Guittard

To: Nancy Labastida

Monday, November 29, 2021, at 1:06 p.m.

Most of what I need to do to clear out the apartment but there is still stuff on the floor and that is depressing. All of it will be better tomorrow but I am sitting here in [it] today. I wish I had my partner here with me, but if wishes were horses, beggars would ride.

Nancy Labastida

To: Charles Guittard

November 29, 2021, at 1:09 p.m.

I'm sorry that the situation is depressing for you. I wish I could be there to help or at least give moral support.

Charles Guittard

To: Nancy Labastida

Monday, November 29, 2021, at 1:26 p.m.

That was not a hint, just a loud groan. You are my moral support, there is no question of that.

Nancy Labastida

To: Charles Guittard

Tuesday, Nov 30, 2021, at 8:00 a.m.

Hahaha. I know it's hard to quit emailing me from that computer. I'm going to miss the emails intensely.

Charles Guittard

To: Nancy Labastida

Tuesday, November 30, 2021, at 8:17 a.m.

Me too, but never say never. I will miss the daily putting my thoughts to you in writing and email makes it so easy to do. But as much as I will miss it, person-to-person communication and accompanying PDA is first priority for this love-smitten guy.

[Charles' note: No emails from December 1–December 11. We were married in Austin, Texas, on Saturday, December 11, 2021.]

PART II

More Disclosure: Albums and an Interview with Young Nancy

My purpose in exchanging albums and other information about each other was multi-fold, but as important as anything else was discovering the young Nancy, the youthful, playful, competitive Nancy that I had missed knowing. I assumed understanding the young Nancy would be helpful, if not the key, to my grasp of the adult Nancy.

In my first meeting with Nancy at her house in Austin, I took photograph albums of me and my family, and Nancy pulled out her albums to supplement the information already shared by email and telephone. Nancy's albums were more voluminous than my own, with lots of pictures and clippings from her days as a competitive junior tennis player. Her trophies as a junior player were numerous and combined with the trophies she won as a senior, are impressive. Not counting all the trophies her mother gave away to aspiring young tennis players, the total number from the several periods of her tennis careers was mind-boggling. Many currently rest on the shelf in the front closet at her home in Austin and others on the bookshelves in the family room along with pictures of The Brentham Club, her tennis club in London, England.

However, of the all-voluminous clippings in her album of clippings, one in particular caught my attention, written by the late legendary sports writer Stan Hochman for the Waco News-Tribune early on in his career while attending the Junior Wightman Cup Tourney matches on the Baylor courts in July 1956 (See Gloria Hochman's entertaining biography, *Stan Hochman Unfiltered: 50 Years of Wit and Wisdom from the Groundbreaking Sportswriter*). Stan Hochman (1928-2015) achieved considerable fame covering the Philadelphia Phillies for the Philadelphia Daily News for over fifty years. My impressions below about young Nancy and interviewer Stan Hochman are based on Hochman's article published Friday, July 20, 1956, which was smack in the middle (age fifteen) of her six years as a junior tennis star. Nancy, if she had her choice of interviewer, could have done no better than Stan Hochman, who was always as interested in an athlete's personality, not just his or her athletic prowess or any drama in the contest he was covering.

The occasion for the interview was a lull between matches just before the semifinal match. Nancy was sitting in the grass waiting for her next opponent to appear when Hochman got Nancy talking. In the informal interview and article that followed, Hochman demonstrated sharp observation of an athlete's physical appearance, noting:

"The bulky, glittering braces on her teeth didn't bother Nancy Davis but a jagged hole in the toe of one her socks did, and she tucked her left foot self-consciously under her right. Miss Davis wriggled restlessly in the shade ... while waiting for her semifinal opponent to arrive ... She rolled over on her stomach, blinked her brown eyes saucily, and said, 'because I only brought two pairs of socks, I thought I'd just be here two days.'"

Nancy, a tennis sensation since she won her first tournament at the age of twelve, had already beaten Jean Johannes on Wednesday and then whipped Virginia Brown of Fort Worth, Texas, two or three years older, in quarter finals. Now she was waiting for her next opponent, Harriet Pullen, two years older than her, to show up for semis. Nancy seemed to be becoming gloomier and gloomier by the minute; she had not expected to still be competing in the prestigious tournament and against older players.

As they talked there in the grass at courtside, Hochman proved also a keen observer of Nancy's emotional state and fidgeting, noting:

"While she waited, she tugged out handfuls of grass and watched them drift slowly down, she sat up and laid down, propped herself on one elbow, crossed and uncrossed her legs, working out the nervous energy."

Hochman also carefully recorded, apparently in a notebook he kept for this purpose, Nancy's language and her way of expressing herself:

"Her language is the brisk vocabulary of a teen-ager and she tumbles the words out between her braces at a breath-taking rate. 'I had a jumbo cheese-burger for lunch and a huge soda. I eat that every day, because I can't afford more, no, that's not true, I can afford more, but that's what I like,' she confessed, then paused for breath."

As the afternoon wore on, Hochman wondered if the fifteen-year-old was getting nervous, Nancy replying that she was not jittery and thought she would stretch out and take a little nap while waiting for Miss Pullen. However, when Miss Pullen arrived, Hochman observed that "Nancy suddenly developed mysterious aches and pains. 'My stomach hurts,' she groaned, 'And I sure don't feel very good.' However, the ailments vanished as she whipped through the first set, 6-1. She had a 3-1 lead in the second set, then fell apart and lost 1-6, 6-4, 6-2. 'I guess I got overconfident,' she shrugged later." [Another reporter] stated that in the Pullen-Davis match "Miss Pullen staged a gallant comeback to defeat Nancy Davis of Dallas in the singles semi-final ... The 15-year-old Miss Davis won the first set easily and held a 3-1 lead in the second set before Miss Pullen started her rally."

Looking at that clipping once more, it was obvious to me that Stan Hochman was quite taken with the young Nancy, her "pixie sense of humor," self-confidence, competitiveness, and her uninhibited chattiness, all qualities inherited by the adult Nancy emailing the adult Charles. Reporting on the Junior Wightman Cup in Waco, Texas, was likely not a coveted assignment for a young sportswriter, but Stan Hochman elevated the task by his talent and sharp interest in delineating interesting sports characters. Nancy was and is an interesting personality. Stan Hochman's "You are There" interview preserved in that clipping is the only window into the quintessence of the young Nancy, there being no videos or audios.

In the fall of 1956, Charles would return to Hillcrest High School as a ninth grade trombonist and Nancy Davis would return from the summer's competitions for her junior year at Hillcrest. Hillcrest tennis team photos prominently feature Nancy with her racket. Both the Davis and Guittard families continued to play tennis at Northwood Club, but Charles and Nancy never ran into each other.

Charles and Nancy at their keyboards.

Charles screws his courage to the sticking place.

The first 6 a.m. encounter.

"And Then There's The Time That…"

Nancy's Best Stories:
Her Memoir of Growing Up

The author, since meeting Nancy, has heard many, likely not most, of Nancy's stories. You don't have to pump her to hear them; they just come spilling out when almost anything triggers them. It became obvious that her stories are part and parcel of who she is, her personality, and her charm. So, I started making a few notes. Usually, my notes were no more than a few keywords words to trigger our recollections, especially Nancy's. The challenge then was to coax Nancy to provide details for her stories, but then to get her to include this task into her busy social schedule along with her bridge playing sessions and other activities. The dialogue below is representative of our conversations about including her stories as a memoir in this volume. The stories which follow are the result, but no attempt has been made to put them in chronological order.

Charles: So, are you on board to include some of your stories in this book? You need to get these down. Your grandchildren will thank you.

Nancy: Sure, why not? ... Well, I'm not sure ... On second thought, maybe not. Who would get to read them? I may not want to tell everything. There are other people in my stories. I don't want to offend anyone.

Charles: Sure, of course not, that's the reason for editing ... Anything else worrying you?

Nancy: This is also going to take chunks of my time. You disappear into the office for hours while working at your computer. There are people who rely upon me to play bridge with them. Sometimes I have to pick up people who can't drive and then take them back home afterwards, sometimes out of my way. And I have tennis tournaments to watch—that's always been my lifelong passion even though I don't play anymore. Charles, you're the writer—why don't *you* write up my stories? You've heard them all.

Charles: Tell you what. I've picked out what seem to be twenty or so of your best stories. Just type out any needed details in any form or fashion. I'll take it from there, and you can copyedit it. Deal? All I want is ten to twenty pages. The book will be a couple of hundred pages. Your part will be easy-peasy. Okay?

Nancy: Well, Okay. Let's see how it goes.

⎯⎯ •⊙✕⊙• ⎯⎯

Nancy Becomes *Stella Starr*: Her Best Prank

Nancy: This is a story from my SMU days. I was with two close girlfriends, and one was talking about her big crush, Jim B–, who I barely knew. We concocted a plan to play a trick on him. I called Jim, and with my voice lowered about an octave, I told him my name was Stella Starr and that I had seen him and wanted to have a rendezvous with him. His being amenable to the idea, I asked him to meet me at the Casbah. Really!! There was such a place on Knox Street. At the appointed time, my friends and I parked our car at a vantage point and watched Jim go into the Casbah. We left in great hilarity and were thrilled to have succeeded with such a ridiculous plot. It was hard to believe that our trick had worked.

A few days later, we [I] called Jim again, and once more I went into character as Stella Starr. I apologized profusely for standing him up, and we made another date. Jim showed up for the second time, again as we watched from afar. As I got older and wiser, I have always wanted to meet Jim again and reveal the true identity of Stella Starr. I imagine he has wondered who it really was for the last sixty years.

Charles: I remember Jim from my SMU law school days—a smart guy and a good guy. Anything about him suggesting he deserved this sort of prank?

Nancy: No, no, but you are taking this far too seriously. That's what some college students do—they play pranks when a good one occurs to them. Some of us can't help it. I mean, how often does a golden opportunity to play such a prank come along?

Charles: Okay, I've played some pranks, too. Usually not a good idea, but sometimes fun to talk about later.

⸻ ⸺ ⬥⬦⬥ ⸺ ⸻

The Davis Family's Fascination
with Radio's Walking Man Contest

Nancy: The day was March 6, 1948, and the country was gripped with the mania for Ralph Edward's *Truth or Consequences* radio program, as it was every Saturday night. Apart from the game, there was always a mystery person that listeners tried to identify each week. Clues were given, and prizes were added to the jackpot until there was a winner, which usually happened after just a few weeks.

Well, in 1948 the mystery person was called "The Walking Man," who was not identified quickly, and the jackpot grew and grew, and clues were added. The first clue was the sound of walking feet. I'll never forget that sound as long as I live, although I was only six. Listeners had to write a slogan to be considered to be called to guess the identity and win the prizes. The Walking Man contest went on and on and on, week after week; the jackpot grew and grew and grew, and my mother submitted slogan after slogan. Mom was always adept at puzzles involving words, listened to a lot of radio in those days, and was quite gifted. Mom entered slogans under her own name, Betty X Davis, and also under the name of her great aunt, Florence Hubbard, who lived in Chicago. Although Mom was the one who came up with the slogans, Mom thought Aunt Florence had a better chance of being called. I don't know why. Mom and Dad worked very hard at figuring out the clues and were convinced that the man, based on the clues given, was Doak Walker, the SMU football star, and they told Aunt Florence to be sure to say "Doak Walker," if she were to be called.

The jackpot eventually reached a record-breaking number of prizes, which included a Cadillac convertible, a small private airplane, a piano, a washer and dryer, an automatic ironer, a radio and record player console, a diamond and ruby watch, among other things. Finally, there was a giveaway clue, as the contest needed to

225

end. There were three contestants on the line waiting to take their chance at winning the jackpot. The clue made it obvious that the Walking Man was not Doak Walker, but was in fact, Jack Benny! We listened with excitement, as did the rest of the nation, and the first contestant on the line was Florence Hubbard! When Ralph Edwards asked Aunt Florence the identity of the Walking Man, we held our breaths, and she answered it, "Is it Jack Benny?" Ralph Edwards asked her to repeat her answer, and she did, and we went crazy in our living room in Dallas. I vividly remember everything. I threw myself on the floor and rolled around. I could not control my emotions.

Years later, I was talking to a radio talk show host and told him about that night, and he told me he was calling a basketball game that same night, and they stopped the basketball game to announce that the Walking Man contest had been won. It made the headlines in newspapers across the country. My siblings and I were dreaming of riding in the Cadillac convertible and flying in the airplane, but that was not to be. My father went to help Aunt Florence sell those items. Sigh. We did get the other prizes mentioned above though. Aunt Florence was an impeccably dressed and coifed widow who lived in Chicago. After winning the contest, she traveled the country as a spokesperson for the heart association and had a long-lasting friendly relationship with Ralph Edwards. Eventually, she retired and moved to Ft. Lauderdale, Florida. She lived to be ninety-nine years old and spent her last years in Dallas to be near my mother, Betty X Davis, her closest relative.

Charles: Did the Davis family in Dallas get to see any of the prizes from the contest? Did your mother or others ever win any other radio or TV contests? Do you remember any of your mother's slogans? What were they about?

Nancy: Yes, I already mentioned those. The airplane and the Cadillac convertible were sold for cash, and the rest of the items were delivered to us on South Versailles. You can see the piano with all our family gathered around it in that photo on the wall on the left of the TV. And we really used that washer and dryer, automatic ironer, and radio and record player console. I don't remember any specific slogans, but they had to be twenty-five words or less and had to be about the importance of donating to the heart association. Mother was really good at them.

Slow Dancing with the Shy Boy Who Wore Contact Lenses

<u>Nancy</u>: In 1955, Ebb White and I were sophomores at Hillcrest High School and we dated quite often. Ebb was a very friendly boy, but he was a bit shy around girls and was very slow to initiate any advances towards me. We were maybe at the handholding phase, but not kissing yet. One night we went to a formal dance, and I wore my favorite formal dress—which was strapless. It was a hand-me-down from my older sister, Libby—she had worn it before me and then after that we shared it depending on whoever had to wear a formal dress on a particular weekend. The dress itself had a gold lamé top with sequins all around and a white net skirt. That night, Ebb, one of the earliest users of contact lenses at Hillcrest, was wearing contacts rather than his regular glasses, which had been extremely thick. As we were slow dancing that evening, one of his contacts popped out and landed somewhere on the top part of my strapless dress. At that moment, all Ebb cared about was retrieving his precious expensive contact lens, his shyness with girls immediately disappearing as he pawed around my dress top trying to find the lens. As he started to paw my sequined top, I became quickly anxious and modest and grabbed the nearest girl to come to my rescue and take Ebb's place in searching my bodice for the lens, which had blended right in with the clear sequins. We were fortunately able to find the lens and returned it to a relieved Ebb. Ebb and I remained lifelong friends despite this uneasy moment in our relationship.

<u>Charles</u>: Who found the contact?

<u>Nancy</u>: That girl I grabbed. I don't remember her name.

<u>Charles</u>: Where was the contact? Seems like it would have been on the floor.

Nancy: It was caught in the sequins while we were slow-dancing.

Charles: Wish I had had contacts in high school. My lenses were coke-bottle thick, too. I generally took them off for photos.

What Happened with Nancy's First Serious Boyfriend

Nancy: Wally Windom was my boyfriend during my last year at Hillcrest and first year at Highland Park. He was a year ahead of me, funny, and adored me and had a cool car, a 1955 Chevy Impala stick-shift with loud pipes that he let me drive around with my girlfriends. I could really peel out and leave rubber in that thing. That resulted in my getting a ticket from the policeman who pulled me over at our rendezvous location, a Time-Out Drive-In on Hillcrest. Wally also had a group of friends who dated some of my friends, so I had a lot of fun with him for about two years. He fell hard and wanted to marry me, so I went along with that idea. I dreamed about our having a daughter together and that we would name her "Winsome Windom." One of my special talents has always been thinking up names for children, especially those of other people; my priority was always to choose a name that would ensure a person's popularity in high school.

Anyway, Wally and I even visited my father's office at SMU together so that Wally could ask permission to be engaged to me. I was seventeen, and my father said no, that I was still a minor, and I had to obey him. I'm sure it didn't help that Wally had dropped out of Hillcrest and enrolled in what some of the Hillcrest kids unkindly referred to as "Mrs. Parker's School for Idiots," where he obtained his GED. About that time, Wally also lost his driver's license because of too many speeding tickets and joined the Marines, with me promising to wait. I knew I did not love him, but I was going to marry him anyway because I didn't want to hurt his feelings.

One summer he was home on leave from the Marines and was driving his car. Wally said his Marine gunny sergeant had told him that since he was in the military, he could go ahead and drive his car although he had lost his license. We agreed that he would drive me to Waco, Texas, to a tennis tournament I was entered to play in. Apparently, being in the Marines had not affected Wally's driving habits and, on the way down, a trooper pulled us over for speeding. The trooper took Wally into Hillsboro to jail and I, on the other hand, drove Wally's car to the tournament in Waco. I had my driver's license. His mother drove to Hillsboro and took him back to Dallas. I did well in the Waco tournament, and a newspaper article featuring an interview with me by the still unknown sportswriter Stan Hochman appeared in the Waco News-Tribune. That article is excerpted elsewhere in this book.

Well, I was seventeen and started SMU soon after Wally left. At SMU, I got the freshman rush and realized I could never marry Wally. I had to break up with him, which I did. His mother was so upset that she called my best friend to talk about the breakup. My friend stopped talking to me for a short time, until I convinced her to reconsider. Eventually, Wally came back from the Marines, and at a welcome home party, he reconnected with another close friend of mine, and they got married. I was very happy about that, although the mother of my close friend who married Wally was extremely upset at her daughter's marriage to Wally. Wally ultimately turned out to be a pretty good guy, and so far as I know, he was a good husband. He did do one thing that might have proved to be a fly in the ointment where our relationship was concerned. He called me up at my SMU sorority house after I participated in a civil rights sit-in at the Greyhound bus station in downtown Dallas. He was angry at my support of civil rights and called me an "N-lover."

Charles: You say you liked to think up names for children. When you had your first child with Fernando, why didn't you name him something else like, Lincoln Labastida or Lorenzo Labastida? How about Leonardo Labastida? Those would have been pretty popular. By my count, there are at least four Fernando Labastidas for genealogists to keep straight so far.

Nancy: Charles, the answer is when I married Fernando Labastida, I adopted Mexican traditions. His father was a Fernando, and our first son (Fernando Augusto) and first grandson (Fernando Xavier) were also named Fernando. If the last [Fernando] has a son, he will be named Fernando something and he will be the fifth Fernando. It's a done deal.

Charles: I'll always be grateful I wasn't named Clarence after my father. That's a questionable first name for a boy. I didn't even have a cool song named after me like Fernando. How about your first name? How do you feel about being named Nancy Davis?

Nancy: I've gotten used to it; I was named after my paternal grandmother. The Nancy fad started after Nancy Sinatra and Ronald Reagan's wife, Nancy Davis Reagan, were in the news. When I added Labastida, my name became unusual at last.

Nancy's Eureka Discovery of the Pronunciation of the Word "Prejudice"

Nancy: I was an avid reader as a kid, and when I came across a written word I had never seen, I pronounced it according to the rules I learned in my spelling lessons in grade school. I came across the word *prejudice* several times. I pronounced it in my head as *pre-JEW-dice*, with the accent on the second syllable, and the *I* pronounced as a long *I* with a silent *E*. I suppose I guessed at the meaning in the context of the book or newspaper I was reading. I actually was very familiar with the spoken word *prejudice* without knowing how to spell it, as I was against racial prejudice ever since I can remember. One day it dawned on me that *pre-JEW-dice* was prejudice! I think there were other similar situations of a disconnect, but that is the one that stands out most in my memory.

Nancy Sings "Jingle Bells" Hoping for a Bike

I was probably seven years old when a brand-new Sears was built in Dallas on deep south Greenville Avenue near the intersection with Ross. It was opened with great fanfare and publicity, and my mother and I saw that there were contests for kids with the grand prize being a new bicycle. I had been yearning for a bicycle for a long time, so I began dreaming of winning one at Sears. Mom took me to Sears the morning of the opening to enter me in the contest for children my age, which was an egg in spoon race. I won the race! All the children who had won the contests of their age group were to come back in the afternoon to the final competition for the bicycle. I was really pumped. Competition was in my blood, and I was a winner, at least in athletic competitions.

The afternoon competition, however, was to see who could sing "Jingle Bells" the best. Even though I did not think of myself as a singer, I went home and practiced and practiced. Mom coached me on how to smile and make my eyes sparkle and show poise on the stage. I suppose there were ten or twelve competitors. The youngest was a little girl of about two or three—yes, two or three! —and she was dressed as a canary in a bright yellow snow suit. The emcee made a big deal about her and called her a little canary and carried on and on about her. She could barely talk, much less sing Jingle Bells, but when she managed a few lines, the crowd went wild. I knew at that moment that I was not going home with a new bicycle that day. The tiny canary won the big two-wheeler bike, which she wouldn't be able to ride for years. I still can get worked up if I think about it.

Charles: Couple of questions. How did you make your eyes sparkle? As to the little girl in yellow winning, how did that go down with you and your mom? When did you finally get a bike? Did you have to sing for it?

Nancy: It's easier to show you than to explain it *(she makes her eyes wide, blinks, and smiles)*. As to the little canary winning, I was broken-hearted, but my parents gave me a bike in time. I got better.

Charles: No seven-year-old wants to lose to a three-year-old.

Nancy: It was humiliating, for sure. Why don't you ask me about all the tennis tournaments and swimming competitions I won? I was a star tennis player in high school and as a senior in London!

Charles: Yes, yes, your collection of trophies is impressive, I admit. And all those tennis rackets on the utility bathroom walls.

Nancy: (*laughing*) I don't like to brag, but you made me.

Nancy's Former Boyfriend Reneges on a Gift She Loved

Nancy: During my SMU years, I dated Kenny M–, a boy I knew from Hillcrest. Kenny was a maverick; he could be a tough guy, and he had a "bad" reputation, but he always treated me well. One time he gave me a record player, which I loved, and I played my records constantly, especially while studying. I went out of town one weekend, and when I got back, my record player was missing. I asked my younger siblings if they knew what happened. One of them told me that Kenny had just walked in the front door, gone upstairs to my room, and taken the record player, and then left without saying anything to anyone. Kenny and I were no longer dating then, but I was very upset at his theft of my record player which I loved. When I called him to demand an explanation, he told me that he had to get the record player to pay off a poker game debt.

Charles: Did you ask him to win it back for you, since it was yours?

Nancy: (*laughing*) No. We were no longer dating and that would have had a fat chance.

Another Good Party Was All Set for the Como Motel

Nancy: During the summer before starting SMU, I played my last season of junior tournaments. I was beginning to realize that I needed to break up with Wally Windom, who was away with the Marines. I had begun a romance on the tennis tournament circuit with Weston Wolff, a nice guy from Odessa, Texas, who was headed to Texas Tech on a tennis scholarship. The last tournament of the summer was in Waco. I remember my younger brother Harvey being there, and my friend Karen S– came to Waco to watch me play. We were staying in a motel in Waco, as were many other young tennis players, including Weston Wolff. On the last night there, a group of us got together in one of the rooms and told jokes and laughed, flirted, cuddled, and stayed up all night, having innocent fun. Weston and I fell in love then.

Summer ended, and I started my freshman year at SMU. Weston and the tennis team from Texas Tech were coming to SMU for a match. One of the boys on the team and my friend Karen had a little flirtation in Waco, and she wanted to see him again. We wanted to recreate the fun we had in Waco, so we hatched a plan. Weston was staying at the Como Hotel in Dallas, and Karen and I wanted to join him and his friend for another all-nighter. Karen and I went out that night on a double date; I was with Weston, and Karen was with a local boy. I told my parents that I was spending the night with Karen, and Karen told her mother she was spending the night with me. There were two major problems with our clever plan. The first was that Weston's friend was coming separately to Dallas and didn't know where Weston was staying, so Karen left a message with her father that if the boy called, he should tell him that Weston was staying at the Como Motel.

The second problem was that my mother called Karen's mother to invite Karen's parents to a party, and thus they discovered our deceit! We concocted some story to Karen's innocent date so that he would drop off Weston, Karen and me at the Como Motel. As we drove up, we saw Karen's father in his big Cadillac waiting for us in front of the motel! We were mortified, and as we got in the car, he asked, "Is Scooter in on this?" Scooter was Karen's friend and had no knowledge of the escapade.

<u>Charles</u>: What did your parents say when they found out about this incident? How many times were you grounded growing up?

Nancy: Sadly, the result of that night was that I was grounded indefinitely, and my "love" for Weston just went dead cold. It was over.

Charles: How did you pick the Como Motel for your party? It's reputation in Dallas wasn't that good. Pretty sleazy place, I think.

Nancy: Karen and I didn't pick it—Weston Wolff did for his stay in Dallas—it was cheap. By the way, this all happened way before that rendezvous you seem to have in your mind between Candace Montgomery and Allan Gore that led up to Candace Montgomery chopping up Betty Gore. That was in the late 1970s.

Too Much Roy Rogers?

Nancy: Linda Haire was the most popular girl I'd ever known, and she lived right across the street from us on Churchill Way. I liked girls who were popular. That's what popularity does for high school students. People like them. One thing about Linda that everybody didn't know was that she was crazy, madly in love with singing cowboy movie star Roy Rogers and everything about Roy Rogers—Roy, Dale Evans (Roy's singing cowboy wife), Trigger (Roy's horse), Buttercup (Dale's horse), Nellie Belle (the ranch jeep), and Bullet (Roy's dog). Linda had stacks and stacks of Roy Rogers comic books in her room and had posters of Roy Rogers and Trigger; Roy Rogers and Dale Evans; and Roy Rogers, Dale Evans, and Trigger all over her room. For Linda, it was everything Roy Rogers every day all day long.

One day when I was probably eleven years old, Linda and I were chatting in her bedroom, which was almost a shrine to Roy Rogers. There in that holy shrine to Roy Rogers, for reasons unknown, I popped off and said, "I hate Roy Rogers," and Linda quietly answered, "I hate you, too." I immediately knew I had made a big mistake by attacking Roy Rogers, a figure beloved by all Americans. Linda was sweet and lovely and never said anything mean to anybody. Roy Rogers was a good guy, too, for that matter. Dale loved him and probably Trigger did and Bullet too. I'll never forget my mortification, but we put it behind us and carried on as usual. I was seldom in Linda's orbit, as she was several years older, and she continued to be super popular and was elected homecoming queen at Hillcrest.

Charles: I read somewhere recently that the Roy Rogers Museum was closing. I wonder how Linda would feel about that.

Nancy: That's a good question. Why don't you ask her? I wouldn't dare. Actually, she's no longer with us.

Maybe a City Girl Shouldn't Try to Ride a Horse Without Instruction

Nancy: Another time on Churchill Way, my sister Libby and I wanted a horse more than anything in the world, which was one of the motivations for my parents to buy a house on Churchill Way—which then was to say "out in the country." Eventually, we got a horse named Lady. On the day we got the horse, Daddy left his office at SMU to go to Fair Park to rent a horse trailer, then he went to get the horse and left it in our field, went back to Fair Park to return the horse trailer, and was en route back to his office. Before he actually got back to his office, I had come home from school, saddled and mounted Lady, but then fell off and broke my arm.

Charles: Did your arm hurt?

Nancy: Darn sure did. The nurse that fixed it gave me three injections intended to numb my arm and then manipulated the bones into place. Hurt like hell, actually. When I broke my arm a second time another day, they put me to sleep, and it didn't hurt at all while they were fixing it.

Charles: Did Lady buck you off?

Nancy: No, that would make a better story. I fell off when the saddle started sliding. I didn't really know how to saddle a horse and must have botched the saddling.

Maybe Nancy Shouldn't Have Tried This, Either

Nancy: When I was six or seven, during which my family was going through hard times, my father gave me a shiny 50-cent piece, which was more money than I had ever had at that time. For reasons that I cannot fathom now, I swallowed the coin. I had to confess what I had done to my father, who was not well pleased. Money was really precious in those days. Eventually, of course, we got the 50-cent piece back through nature's way. I never saw it again. Daddy kept it.

Charles: Didn't you ask your father for the return of the 50-cent piece? I thought it was yours to do with it whatever you wanted to with it.

Nancy: No, I didn't. That would have been unthinkable! You didn't know Daddy.

Maybe a Dog Shouldn't Try to Eat a Chicken in One Gulp

Nancy: Also on Churchill Way, we lived in a house set on three acres with a barn and a chicken house. At one point, my little sister, Virginia, got a dog. Shortly after his arrival on Churchill Way, he raided the chicken house and ate a chicken. That was curtains for the dog. My parents, along with Virginia, drove the dog straight to the pound to return him. On the drive, Virginia and the dog were in the back seat. During the dog's last ride, he vomited the chicken all over Virginia. The good news for Virginia was that my parents bought her a new dress.

Charles: I guess the old dress wasn't cleanable.

Nancy: I think it was the idea of the old dress that was the problem.

• • • • • •

Nancy's Great Moment as a Civil Rights Activist; She Loses Some Friends

Nancy: When I was a junior at SMU, I participated in the first sit-in in Dallas, and it was one of the high points of my life, having been against racial segregation since my earliest memories. I was living on campus at the Chi Omega house, and I belonged to the Young Democrats Club at SMU. One of the other members of the Young Democrats called to ask if I would participate in a sit-in at the Greyhound bus station, and I was thrilled to be able to do that. SMU's undergraduate school was still segregated (it was 1960); however, the graduate schools were integrated by that time. Two black theology students were planning to take a Greyhound bus home for the Thanksgiving holidays. At the station, they attempted to eat at the lunch counter and were refused service, even though there was a federal law prohibiting discrimination in interstate travel by bus, train, or plane. The two students went back to SMU and contacted known liberal students to organize a sit-in. I went along with several others to a Black church to be prepped on how to act and what to do at the sit-in.

We white students as instructed sat in a booth at the bus station with a Black student, and when the waitress came to take our order, we asked if she would serve our friend. When she refused, we refused to either order or leave. The waitress chose my booth to try to take an order, and I had to be strong and brave and ask if she would serve all of us and then decline to order unless for all of us. She came to my booth three times, and each time it was the same. We had a predetermined time at which we would all stand up and leave. We left as planned. Outside, there were news reporters with cameras. When I got back to the sorority house, I wanted to watch the news, and there I was on film, leaving the bus station. One of my sorority sisters saw me and said, "Your pin should be jerked," and flounced out of the room. I was overjoyed. I did get an anonymous phone call calling me a "N— lover."

Charles: Were you nervous sitting in the Greyhound lunch counter? I would have been. Were you afraid you might be arrested, and what was your parents' reaction? When my roommate and I lodged a written protest at Baylor over President McCall's closing of *Long Day's Journey into Night*, the Dean of Men sent a letter of complaint to my mother. Mother was upset.

Nancy: Mother and Daddy weren't upset. They were rather proud of me, as it reflected their values. Why was your mother upset? Wasn't she proud of you?

Charles: Mother was always super-cautious. I think she thought getting crosswise with the president of the university was not a good move for a young man trying to rise in the world. Father, on the other hand, didn't seem to be bothered at all. He was apparently reminded of his own days at Baylor when he stood up on one occasion to President Neff's autocratic ways as president.

Nancy: If I had gone to Baylor, I would have definitely wanted to protest the closing of the play with you. Maybe we could have had a sit-in at the Baylor cafeteria.

Charles: Or stand-in at the president's office.

Nancy and Cheaters in Competitive Games

Nancy: I have zero respect for cheaters. Also, everyone knows who the cheaters are. What's the point? Where is that glorious feel-good feeling of winning if you had to cheat to get that trophy or those accolades? When I was a young girl playing in tournaments around Texas, I often heard of an adult lady who played the tournaments who cheated, and everyone knew it and talked about it. Her name was Tricky Trixie [not her real name]. I never forgot that name. More than forty years later, I played in a senior tournament in Texas, and there was Tricky Trixie playing in the eighty-year-old category. People were still talking about her cheating. I've seen people cheat in bridge, also. It's rare in bridge

238

games, which makes it all the more shocking and perplexing. I've heard about cheating in the highest ranks of bridge players. The penalties are severe, and the shame is worse. What a hollow victory to win by cheating!

Charles: What do you do, or did you do, when someone you are playing against at tennis or bridge tries to cheat?

Nancy: In the live bridge games I play in now, no one cheats, and we are all friends who wouldn't think of cheating. In the games online where I'm playing with people all over the world, occasionally I suspect someone of cheating—sending signals to their partner—but it doesn't happen too often. It is possible to wage a complaint with the online tournament director, but I've never done it.

Scary Girls in the Neighborhood

Nancy: When Libby and I were probably ages eight and six and lived on South Versailles, we took our little sister Virginia, age three, out for a walk. We walked down Roland Avenue crossing two streets and headed to Edmondson Park at Beverly Drive. We arrived at the corner of Beverly and Roland when we spotted two sisters on the other side of Beverly where they lived. The sisters, several years older than we were, were in their Catholic school uniforms. For some unknown reason, Libby and I had built up in our minds an irrational fear of running into those two sisters, and that day when we saw them there in our path to the park, our worst fears had finally come true. Panicking, we dropped little Virginia's hands and ran home as fast as we could, leaving our baby sister to fend off the two menacing sisters by herself. A few minutes later, the sisters appeared at our door with Virginia, holding her hand, bringing her safely back home. To this day, I don't understand why we felt what we felt or did what we did.

Charles: You've had a lot of time to think about that incident. Nothing further comes to mind about how it could have occurred?

Nancy: Nothing really, but there was sort of an echo chamber effect on any emotion Libby or I felt, as we were very close in those years. And we both had over-active imaginations.

How Betty X Davis Got Her X

Nancy: My mother was christened Elizabeth Test—no middle name. Mom was always called Betty. When Mom was in high school, she and a good friend, who also had no middle name, decided to give themselves middle names. My mother must have thought long and hard and finally came up with her solution—Xenophen. She used that middle name for years. When I was in school and asked to fill out my parents' names, I would carefully write down *Elizabeth Xenophen Test Davis.* I remember doing that many times. Eventually, Mom decided that Xenophen was pretentious and was a name for a man so she dropped it, all except for the X. She was known far and wide as Betty Davis and had to field countless references to Bette Davis, plus there were many, many Betty Davises around; there were four in our church, for example. Therefore, Mom kept the X and legally changed her name to Betty X Davis, essentially to distinguish her from all the other thousands of Betty Davises!

Charles: I couldn't find Xenophen when I Googled it; I did find Xenophon. The name Xenophon is supposedly a gender-neutral name meaning "strange voice." It was also the name of a Greek philosopher. Good that Betty X eventually settled for an X. You had your own problem being Nancy Davis.

Nancy: (*laughing*) For sure. However, when I married Fernando in 1964 and became Nancy Davis Labastida, I solved that problem. Betty Davis and Nancy Davis were both such popular names.

Charles: Yes, but I had to practice saying your name over and over so I wouldn't introduce you as Nancy *Labatista*. The names are so similar. It took me months. I had the name of that Cuban dictator guy Batista in my head. I think he was a bad dude.

Nancy: Too bad Cuba has had such troubles. It would have been an interesting place to visit.

The Only Time Betty X Cried

Nancy: My mother lived to the age of one hundred and six years, and the only time I remember her crying was the day that she came upstairs to my room in their house on Rosedale and saw how messy it was. She was sixty-ish at the time, threw herself on the bed, and just sobbed inconsolably. I stared in shock and disbelief, as I was already out of college and working, although living at home. My father was cross with me for upsetting my mother! I moved out the next day and got a little efficiency apartment in the same building where Libby and her husband, Bob, lived. I don't think my parents even realized I was gone until later. They were far too busy with tennis, TV, crossword puzzles, SMU, and my younger siblings.

Charles: Your mom was so even-tempered while you were growing up, despite some challenges, it is hard to understand her emotions on this occasion. Maybe an accumulation of some sort was brewing, and your room that day triggered the teapot finally going off.

Nancy: I have no idea. She did go through a lot and had a very high boiling point. Daddy, on the other hand, had a low boiling point, and I was always afraid of it going off.

Nancy and the "Incubator Baby"

Nancy: In my first-grade class at Bradfield Elementary, I had a little friend named Carolyn Calvin, and she was very popular. I was sure the name helped. If I had been named Daisy Davis or Darcie Davis, that would have been very popular and not as common as Nancy Davis, which name I think I said I got from my paternal grandmother. Also, Carolyn was very small and cute and had her hair in ringlets every day and was an only child whose parents doted on her. Her parents were also older than the other parents. I was just a bit jealous of Carolyn Calvin, but I liked her and loved going to her house to play. I was quite aware of how much smaller she was than me, and I pondered the difference in our sizes a great deal. Then one day, I had a sudden realization that I was very sure I knew why Carolyn was so tiny while I was larger. I could hardly wait until I would see her parents again so that I could confirm my theory. When the big moment came, I ran up to them and asked, "Mrs. Calvin, was Carolyn an incubator baby?" They both just threw back their heads and laughed. I was very disappointed to find out that the clever idea I had come up with was wrong.

Charles: After that, were you later able to discover any small children who were incubator babies?

Nancy: No. There had to be some out there, though.

Daddy and the Airport Exit Difficulty

Nancy: Within the Davises, this story may be the favorite. According to my brother Talbot, Harvey and Betty X went to the airport to collect Talbot and his friend, who were returning home from a tennis tournament. Talbot was fifteen, the age he says when the very existence of one's parents is an embarrassment. Upon entering the car park, one must take a ticket from a machine. My father, who was driving, reached for the ticket and impatiently mangled the tearing of the ticket from the machine. As a result, he came away with only part of it. An hour later when he presented the ticket at the exit booth, the attendant said he couldn't take it like that and that he would have to charge the maximum fee, which would have been much more expensive than the minimum. My father insisted that he only owed the minimum. The attendant said rules are rules and that Daddy couldn't leave until a supervisor could be consulted. Daddy had no interest in waiting for, or pleading his case to, the attendant's supervisor, and just roared on through, shattering the exit arm and declaring, "I'll sue you for false imprisonment." I suspect his claim for false imprisonment would have gone up in flames had he pursued it, which he did not. The fact that he was not only a lawyer but also taught law probably would have resulted in a judgment against him for the car park's attorney's fees and the cost of repair of the exit arm.

Charles: Since the car park probably had your father's license plate number, I would have thought he would have heard back from them, at least with a bill for the destroyed exit arm.

Nancy: That makes sense, but if it ever happened, he and Mom never let on to us kids.

Daddy's Admonition Not to Feel Sorry for Losing Tennis Opponents

Nancy: My parents taught me and all my siblings how to play tennis. Since I showed some promise, my father went beyond the basics and occasionally imparted words of wisdom to me, often based on his own experience. Very early in my tennis life, he warned me against ever feeling sorry for any opponent who I was beating love and love. On one occasion, he said he made the mistake of giving away a courtesy game to ease the pain of an opponent and help him save a little face. One time when he was playing a match and was ahead 6-0, 5-0, he decided to let the poor guy on the other side of the net win just one game, a courtesy game, and then my father would close it out at 6-0, 6-1. Unfortunately, that courtesy game was all the "poor" fellow needed to gain hope and confidence, and he went on to beat my father in three sets.

Charles: Ouch! Have you followed your father's advice in your matches?

Nancy: I've never given anyone a courtesy game, but not just because of his advice. I don't think people want courtesy games when they are being slaughtered. They cheapen the game, so I don't do it, and don't want any myself.

When Nancy Learned Her First Bad Word

Nancy: Mom and Daddy were performing in a play at a local church. One day I went to watch them. In the play, Daddy was changing cars on a train and the plotline had him falling forward into the arms of someone who would catch him. It made me nervous to watch him fall, and I was only four. What I remember best about the play was a single line in the play, the scene lost to my memory, in which one of the players tells the others, "I'm a-coming like hail." I liked this line and repeated it many times starting when I was five; it made my mother laugh and then my family laugh and so I kept saying it— "I'm a-coming like hail." It was not until years later, ten years actually, sitting in a class at SMU that I realized that I was not saying "I'm a-coming like *hail*" but "...like *hell*." Until then, I was always mystified but somehow gratified by my parents' laughter.

Charles: Ten years, wow. Was "hell" the only cuss word you learned by accident?

Nancy: Insofar as I remember, so help me, Hepzibah.

Charles: You were never a Girl Scout?

Nancy: Nope, only a Brownie.

November 22–24, 1963

Nancy: On November 22, 1963, I woke up full of excitement, but also with a feeling of dread and anxiety. President John F. Kennedy and his stunning wife, Jackie Kennedy, were coming to Dallas! They were scheduled to arrive at Love Field airport and then take a motorcade through downtown Dallas, headed to the Trade Mart to speak at a luncheon. Late in the morning Father was already at the Trade Mart, along with other Dallas Democrats. I was working downtown at the Dallas Public Library and asked permission for the 12:00-1:00 lunch hour the minute I arrived at work. I was uneasy about the president's visit to Dallas because the atmosphere in

Dallas was thick with open hatred of him and all Democrat politicians. Adlai Stevenson, a prominent Democrat defeated for president by President Eisenhower, had been spat on and hit with political placards during a recent visit to Dallas.

Successful with my lunch hour request, at 12:00 I rushed out of the library and walked the short distance and positioned myself at the corner of Akard and Main Street, hoping to get a good look at Mrs. Kennedy. Soon, the motorcade was in sight, and I was a bit disappointed to note that I was on the side of the street that had a view of President Kennedy. Mrs. Kennedy was waving to folks on the other side of the street. It was a brilliantly sunny day, and as the motorcade passed, I got a full glorious view of the president, and it felt like he waved right at me. As soon as the motorcade was out of sight, I dashed back to the library to call my mother and report my exhilarating experience and to ask if my father had gotten off okay for his trip to the Trade Mart. While I was talking to Mom, she was watching television and saw the assassination. We both started crying and sobbing. The library was empty except for the people who worked there, and my sobs echoed off the walls and were heard by many people on the second floor of the library. Soon, people started hearing and spreading the news, and library employees were walking around the near empty library crying and sobbing out loud. It was the saddest day of my life for many, many years.

However, although the Dallas police had quickly found and arrested Lee Harvey Oswald, the tragic episode triggered by the assassination of President Kennedy was not over. My job at the library was in the children's room, which was on the southeast corner of the second floor. The windows had a direct view of the Dallas Police Station, which was catty corner to the library and was where Oswald was being held. It was Saturday, November 23, and Oswald was expected to be transferred to the county jail. I had to go work, but there were very, very few children going to the library that day, so I spent almost the entire day looking out the window at all the news cameras and journalists and the excitement in front of the police station. Oswald was not moved that day. The next morning, Sunday, November 24, Mom and I went to church, and while we were there, we heard the news that Oswald had been shot. It was another horribly shocking and tragic day in Dallas.

<u>Charles</u>: My input to your story is that my parents and I heard the news just outside our church from Judge Ed Gossett, a criminal court judge and courthouse colleague of my father. I don't think we knew the assassin was Jack Ruby, owner of the Carousel Club, a Dallas strip club, and police hanger-on, until later that day. As I recall, Ruby told law enforcement his motivation was to save Mrs. Kennedy from the trauma she would have experienced if she had to return for the trial of Oswald. It seems that both Oswald and Ruby had led very troubled lives starting when they were juveniles.

Egged on by her friends, Nancy plays her most satisfying prank.

Nancy contemplates her 50-cent coin.

Nancy sings at Sears Roebuck store for a Christmas bike.

A highway trooper stops Nancy and her boyfriend.

The Trial of J. Hiram Harmless:
A Fantasy of A Final Judgment Day

"Dr. Trang or Dr. Zhiang, Report to OR, *STAT!*" The voice blasted repeatedly over the intercom, gradually waking me, J. Hiram Harmless, on my hospital bed. Then, within a minute or so, my bed, or gurney, banging through double doors after double doors and lurching around hall corners, the pungent smell of hospital bleach and Odo-X so strong it was hard to breathe, the OR doors finally appearing.

A woman, obviously an immigrant physician from the land of Fu Manchu, looked me over perfunctorily for about two seconds. "Groin," she said loudly into a microphone. Then minions of this woman appeared, roughly grabbing and tossing me onto an OR bed.

A blinding overhead light flashed on, and, as I attempted to accustom myself to my new surroundings, I could hear the OR team members laughing and bantering maniacally about their plans for happy hour after work with their girlfriends du jour.

After another fifteen or thirty minutes, or maybe an hour—someone had taken my watch and therefore I could make no accurate estimate of the time—the light dimmed and I could feel myself moving again, this time still on the rolling OR bed. My bed and I whizzed down a dimly lit hall, past portraits of men in dark business suits and shiny ties smiling benignly.

Another door opened and I was rolled into a large domed stadium with palm trees and other vegetation surrounding the largest organ I'd ever seen. Never seen an organ with that many pipes. More than the Mormon Tabernacle in Salt Lake City.

The rolling bed stopped at some point near the center of the hall. A large hospital machine, a sort of Hoyer sling, seized me and dropped me into a large, uncomfortable metal chair. Once in the chair, I noted the inscription on a plaque over the chair which read, "He, for whom the Moment of Ultimate Judgment has come."

As I had supposed I was only in the hospital for another heart stent, which insofar as I was aware would not involve final judgment, the words on the plaque were troubling.

I immediately began rethinking my long-held belief that I had always been a good, although not perfect, specimen of the human race and that being eternally damned was the least of my worries. After all, I had committed no acts of violence toward men, women, or children. No egregious breaches of the Ten Commandments or the Boy Scout Law. In other words, no serious dings on my permanent record that my high school counselor used to talk about.

I began noticing the confusing smells in the stadium. On the one hand, I could detect the fragrant aromas of the beautiful orchids and roses all around. On the other hand, I could swear that a whiff of burning sulfur was also wafting my way, seemingly from an immense pit in the floor of the stadium. A worrisome flickering reddish glow illuminated this pit, and a hand-written sign nearby claimed, *"Don't believe the hype—it's not as bad as it looks—Lucifer."*

As I was pondering whether what I had heard all my life about hell was just "hype" by preachers marketing heaven vs. hades to increase church membership, a tall, thin man in a shiny gold suit climbed into position on the organ. Soon I could hear him playing, "On Christ the solid rock I stand, All other ground is shifting sand." There was also a ghostly choir behind the organ, filling the room with their voices in an eerie harmony.

Simultaneous with the final strains of the hymn's melody, from what I had supposed to be a skylight in the ceiling, a long step ladder descended to a wooden platform near the organ. Two enormous figures stepped off onto the platform. A thunderous amped-up voice reminding me of Laurence Olivier's recorded message at the Parthenon intoned: "All RISE for the Panel—the Lord God Jehovah, Yahweh-Sabaoth; Jesus Christ of Nazareth, the Messiah and Son of God; and the Holy Spirit, the Enabler and Anointer."

The first two figures seated themselves in large thrones, Jehovah in the throne in the middle and Jesus Christ on his right, and the third figure—wherever it was as it was completely invisible— apparently seated itself on the third throne. Standing near the third throne was a magic slate or tablet on an easel for easy access by the Holy Spirit.

Although I cannot describe the appearance of the Holy Spirit, the appearance of the first two members of the Panel is impossible to forget. Jehovah had the look of someone used to taking charge of meetings and yet had a kindly expression on his face. You could tell that although kind, he would not put up with any nonsense in any proceeding he presided over. He was dressed in a Western shirt that snapped up the front and Lee jeans and boots and had already removed his broad-rimmed Stetson as appropriate for a gathering of this gravity. Estimated Resistol hat size, 9½.

Then Jesus Christ looked exactly like he did when he posed somehow for that framed portrait hanging in Sunday school classrooms all over the world. Jesus seemed very comfortable in his long flowing robe, comfortable too with Jehovah taking the lead.

As I waited for the proceeding to start, Jehovah and Jesus seemed to be chatting privately about the matter before them, sometimes in the direction of the third chair, presumably concerning the procedure to govern the Hearing on Final Judgment in the matter of my immortal soul and its destination for all eternity. The following is my best attempt to remember the details of the proceeding for, for better or for worse.

Jehovah: (*sprightly with a twinkle*) Good morning.

Let the record reflect that Robert H. Jackson, former highly respected former U.S. Chief Counsel at Nuremberg and Justice on the U.S. Supreme Court, upon oral motion made and granted, will be appearing for the committee. The committee has alleged charges that will upon conviction bar Mr. Harmless from entering heaven, citing numerous grounds. Mr. Clarence Darrow, former counsel for Loeb & Leopold, John T. Scopes, and numerous other defendants deserving universal censure if not eternal damnation, will be appearing for Mr. Harmless.

Mr. Jackson, the Panel expects this proceeding to run smoothly and swiftly. I hope you do not expect the Panel to relax its rules for this proceeding simply because of your stellar reputation?

Jackson: No, your Honor. Certainly not. I don't expect the Panel to give the prosecution any breaks whatsoever.

Jehovah: And, Mr. Darrow, be warned: that folksy charm which may work for you in other courts is on thin ice before this Panel. We have seen it all since the first soul came before us countless eons ago. We are NOT amused.

Darrow: Touché, your Honor. Point well taken.

Jehovah: *(Ignoring Jackson's and Darrow's ripostes)* Continuing, Mr. Jackson, as you and Mr. Darrow are aware, the Panel met earlier to become familiar with the numerous grounds the review committee has brought against Mr. Harmless. We have concluded that while some of the stated grounds are meritorious and deserve our attention, many of the others do not. In that respect, the Panel agrees with Mr. Darrow. The indictment, therefore, is dismissed as to the following charges:

Charge 3: *Failure to pray daily for the forgiveness of sins.* Mr. Jackson, we doubt even you do this.

Charge 4: *Failure to tithe throughout Mr. Harmless' entire life.* Regrettable, but not exactly a spiritual felony.

Charge 5: *Failure to read the Bible daily.* Also regrettable, but not a spiritual felony.

Charge 8: *Failure to give thanks at mealtimes* with his family by way of the blessing or otherwise. Very common and not a capital offense.

Jehovah: Jesus, did I get that right?

Jesus: Yes, Heavenly Father. So, let it be written, let it be done. Charges 3, 4, and 5 are therefore dismissed.

Jehovah: That leaves us to consider the following felonies: First and foremost,

Charge 1, Mr. Harmless' failure to ever request forgiveness in a serious matter or to ask to be saved from his sinful nature.

In plain language, Mr. Harmless wishes the Panel to waive the clear requirements of scripture on the basis that he has allegedly lived a life as a good man and moral person and his case did not require, or benefit from, Jesus' Resurrection from the dead. In other words, the Good Samaritan Defense.

Charge 2: Mr. Harmless' failure to make any attempt to evangelize the lost or to save a single soul.

The total count of souls saved by him allegedly stands at zero and, further, he has made no attempts of any kind. That's nada or zilch.

Charge 6: Mr. Harmless' questioning the importance of the doctrine of the Trinity to the average Christian's faith.

This is the heart of the faith and the message of the New Testament. Or am I wrong?

(The Holy Spirit writes slowly on its tablet— "That's the sine qua non! If that goes, it all goes!")

Jehovah: Any more, Jesus? Please speak up if there are any. Any more charges, Holy Spirit? You have that tablet to write on, if you need it.

Jesus: No, Heavenly Father. You have covered it.

(The Holy Spirit writes on its tablet, "No, nothing more.")

Jackson: Point of Order, Jehovah, your Honor, we've submitted some other violations which we are prepared to bring before this Panel.

Jehovah: What other violations are you talking about?

Jackson: Some really important ones, your Holiness. For starters, Mr. Harmless' failure to highlight the sayings of your son Jesus in his New Testament, his doodling on church programs, and repeatedly sleeping during sermons. Secondly, telling a supposedly funny Baptism story, over and over again, that he says he witnessed in a church in Dallas, Texas. Yes, it's a funny story, but he shouldn't have told it over and over.

Finally, Mr. Harmless has, since childhood, been more enthusiastic about receiving presents at Christmas time and seeing what was under the tree for him than either giving presents to others or reading the Christmas story in Luke. No doubt he has also passed these attitudes along to his children and perhaps his grandchildren. Surely that warrants at least a stern rebuke.

Jehovah: Counsel, the time for stern rebukes is long past; we are here for a final disposition of Mr. Harmless' immortal soul. We must decide whether it will participate in a life of glory with the Panel in heaven, the Heavenly Choir, the Heavenly Host, and such of his loved ones who may already be in heaven, or whether he shall be consigned to the fiery pit below us under the cruel domination of that rebellious bastard, Lucifer. You will recall that Lucifer is my ancient enemy since we fought eons ago and my angels chased him and his mutinous angels out of heaven. Input, Jesus? Holy Spirit? Mr. Jackson, your point of order is overruled.

(Jesus and the Holy Spirit signal they are in agreement and wish to move ahead with the proceeding.)

Jackson: Note my exception, your Honor.

Jehovah: Mr. Jackson, you must be aware no one can appeal a ruling of this Panel. Withdraw your exception, or we will immediately take up the subject of your own immortal soul.

Jackson: Exception withdrawn, your Honorable Holiness, and humbly petitioning for your forgiveness.

Jehovah: We will be taking that under advisement for disposition when your case comes before the Panel. Any comment, Mr. Darrow, before Mr. Jackson calls his first witness?

Darrow: Although, at this time we are withholding comment on charges 1, 2 and 6, we certainly applaud the court's dismissal of the remaining charges as being below the dignity of this high court. Mr. Harmless and I are both tickled to have such an astute Panel.

Jackson: Objection, your Honor, to Mr. Darrow's naked attempt to butter up this Panel!

Jehovah: Objection overruled this time. Call your first witness, Mr. Jackson.

Jackson: The committee calls as its first witness the former Mrs. Harmless, now Mrs. Hortense Heedless, who was married to Mr. Harmless for seven years before they split up.

It is conceded that Mrs. Heedless went into a fatal meltdown spiritually after the divorce. She is here on a day pass from the Inferno. If I may request St. Peter to help her up out of the pit, those last few steps up are steep and difficult.

(Mrs. Heedless is escorted up the steps to a chair in a small witness box before the Panel.)

Mrs. Heedless, will you please state your official address and what you do in the Inferno?

Mrs. Heedless: I live in apartment 207 on either the third or fourth circle down in the Inferno, I'm not sure which, it's very smoky down there. My job is to lead prayers to our Supreme Lord Lucifer outside the boiler room. I also lead the chants and occasionally sing a solo when asked to. I used to sing in a Lutheran church.

Jackson: Mrs. Heedless, have I or anyone else promised you anything in exchange for your testimony?

Mrs. Heedless: Nothing except an icy Cherry Coke and, if you like my testimony, one of those battery-operated fans to take back down.

Jackson: Thank you for being so honest with us ... You are familiar with the charges against your ex-husband. Can you provide the Panel with any light on the charges before us?

Mrs. Heedless: I certainly intend to. Get out your pencils. I was married to that man for seven full years, yet I never once saw him open a Bible, pray for forgiveness of anything, or say grace at mealtime. He did occasionally drop pocket change into the collection plate the few times we darkened a church doorway. Oh, one time at church I saw him stand up and pull out a dollar bill and wave it at everybody and say he would put it in the plate if ten other men would do the same ... So, did he tithe?

That's a laugh—of course not!

Jackson: So, did he have to put in his dollar?

Mrs. Heedless: He did not. Only three other men raised their hands.

Jackson: Pass the witness.

Darrow: Mrs. Heedless, thank you for coming today to help the Panel ... Now you have talked about a few things Mr. Harmless didn't do during your marriage. I'm going to ask you about some of those things and also about things he did do. Okay?

Mrs. Heedless: Okay. But you should know Lucifer has his eye on you and knows where you live.

Darrow: Okay, fine. First, I want to ask you if you ever saw Mr. Harmless be kind to strangers, in small ways or big ways.

Mrs. Heedless: Oh, yes, a bleeding heart he was, into a lot of causes that strained our budget over and over. We never had enough to take that trip on the Queen Mary, but that's not why we're here. He's not a tither or a Bible reader or a sayer of grace at mealtimes. In my opinion, he belongs in the Inferno here with me. And, for what it's worth, I don't think he's such a good guy like you are trying to make him out to be. He dumped me—ME—for a girl he met at his seventh high school reunion. Mr. Darrow, Hiram made SOLEMN PROMISES to me in front of a godly preacher man. He made those promises right in front of an organ bigger than that one over yonder. And he promised to ALWAYS be with me! *(The rest is inaudible as Mrs. Heedless seems to be crying.)*

Darrow: And those promises you said he made to you yay long ago are what is making you cry today, Mrs. Heedless?

Mrs. Heedless: Yes, they sure are. Very hurtful they were when he dumped me.

Darrow: Your Honor, I move that this witness's testimony be excluded from the record for her obvious bias. For goodness' sake, she is nursing a decades-old grievance and I reckon has a vested interest in his damnation and transportation to the Inferno. Once she gets him down there, she obviously intends to hector him for all eternity.

Jehovah: Mrs. Heedless' opinion testimony about whether the defendant is a good or bad man and the promises he made is excluded, but the rest will be retained for whatever it is worth ... Do you have any other testimony to offer, Mr. Jackson?

Jackson: We have obtained written affidavits from the pastors at the three churches he attended and offer them as additional proof on the issues of Harmless' failure to tithe, pray or say grace at mealtimes, or read the Bible daily. Do you have any objection, Mr. Darrow?

Darrow: We certainly do object—the Panel has already dismissed those counts.

Jackson: Your Honor, those affidavits also address the remaining counts, namely, Mr. Harmless' failure to ever request forgiveness in a serious matter or to be saved from his sinful nature inherited from Adam who was banished from heaven; his failure to reach out to save lost souls; and finally, his failure to understand or believe in the doctrine of the Trinity.

Jehovah: They are admitted as to the retained counts only. Any other testimony, Mr. Jackson?

Jackson: Yes, one final witness. I call the defendant, J. Hiram Harmless.

Mr. Harmless, I'll remind you that you are under oath. *(Winking at the Panel)* Can you give us the approximate year, if you can, that you think you accepted Jesus Christ as your Lord and Savior? In other words, when did you have your conversion experience, who witnessed it, and what church did it occur in?

Harmless: Mr. Jackson, I will answer your question, but first you tell me whether Jehovah, and the rest of the Panel, are Baptists, Methodists, Presbyterians, Episcopalians, Lutherans, Moravians, Evangelicals, or what they are?

Jackson: Objection, nonresponsive. Please direct the witness to answer the question.

Jehovah: Objection sustained. The witness will answer the question.

Harmless: Insomuch as I am unaware of any member of the Panel being of any particular denomination, I will answer the questions but request permission to explain my answers so that the Panel may understand.

Jehovah: Proceed.

Harmless: There was no precise moment, time, or church associated with my becoming a Christian. There were influences, sure, like my parents and the churches I attended, and my teachers, but no "come to Jesus" moment in a big church in front of a big organ. I was raised a Methodist, perhaps a lukewarm Methodist, I grant you.

Some Methodist churches, you no doubt know, are rather lukewarm when compared to certain other denominations like Southern Baptists, for an example. Sermons are shorter and there tend to be no Wednesday night prayer services or weeklong summer revivals. As a Methodist, I was baptized by sprinkling, not dunking, and I was confirmed around the age of twelve.

When I married Mrs. Heedless, who is or was Baptist, being a Baptist was a requirement of a Baptist church marriage, which meant a public Baptism by immersion, so I did it. But being immersed didn't make me a better person any more than sprinkling did.

(*Looking at Jackson*) Be honest, Mr. Jackson, were you a better person or more committed to your faith after being dunked than before you were dunked? Was the good Samaritan less worthy than the people who today claim to have had conversion experiences and walk the center aisle at church at the pastor's tenth altar call at the urging of their parents?

No, I don't tithe, and neither did my parents or grandparents, good Christians that they were, but then I've taken care of my children, and I have never refused a friend in need or raised my hand in anger to man, woman, or child.

As to the doctrine of the Trinity, I'm open-minded and will listen to anyone who thinks he can explain it without shilly-shallying. My impression upon studying the question is that it was formulated by early church theologians trying to harmonize confusing references to God, Jesus, and other spiritual manifestations in the Bible. But the doctrine, it turns out, is as confusing to me as are the references it is intended to harmonize.

Jackson: No further questions. The committee rests.

Darrow: The defense rests and moves the Panel to dismiss the remaining charges for the obvious reason that they embody the same kinds of legalisms that the pharisees were guilty of and which were damned by Jesus himself.

Jackson: The committee moves for judgment on its charges against Mr. Harmless. The Good Samaritan Defense has never been recognized by this Panel and shouldn't be at this late date.

Jehovah: Does either side wish to make a final argument?

Jackson: No, your Honor. The record before you is clear. Mr. Harmless is clearly guilty as charged. He should be, without further ado or ceremony, dispatched to Hades forthwith where he can enjoy the heat and companionship with Mrs. Heedless for all eternity as he deserves.

Darrow: Mr. Harmless, likewise, feels the record is clear. If Jesus thought the good Samaritan in the parable was destined for the Inferno, he would have said so. In fact, he did not. Your angels should immediately escort Mr. Harmless to heaven to join his family already there.

Jehovah: Since there are no further witnesses, the Panel will now retire and consider their verdict...

With those words echoing in my brain, I woke up in this hospital bed with a dull pain in my groin and grabbed for the plastic urinal hooked over the bed railing. Hazy figures in my dream of an ex-wife, Robert Jackson, Clarence Darrow, and a heavyset fellow in cowboy boots were still swirling in my head. Thank God for this nature call before final judgment could be reached. I know it was only a dream after all, but I don't want to enter any damn Inferno, even in a dream! Maybe two melatonin tablets tonight will help. The ironic thing about all of this is that I, Hiram Harmless, have never been married, never even been engaged. Maybe the dream was a warning not to call that woman who brought the three-bean salad to the church's potluck social. Maybe I need to try out that other church's single adult class for a change. *J. Hiram Harmless*

J. Hiram Harmless on the way to the OR.

J. Hiram Harmless realizes the gravity of his situation.

Wrapping It Up & Two More Stories

<u>Charles</u>: Well, that seems to cover most of what we could, or should, for the sake of our families and innocent (or guilty) third parties, put in a book like this. Anything else we definitely should include, do you think?

<u>Nancy</u>: Like what?

<u>Charles</u>: Like something that wouldn't embarrass our children too badly, but we obviously wouldn't have wanted to mention even to each other early on when we were on our best behavior, trying to make a good impression, like my mother always wanted me to.

<u>Nancy</u>: (*laughing*) What—like what *you* sleep in at night?

<u>Charles</u>: Right. That is somewhat embarrassing. Or how about *your* date at the laundromat with the professor you had a crush on?

<u>Nancy</u>: Yes, that's one I don't usually tell around, but I guess that's a fair trade. Also, I have a question that might be interesting.

<u>Charles</u>: Which is?

<u>Nancy</u>: Do you think if we had met each other and dated before we married our first spouses, we would have changed history?

<u>Charles</u>: Maybe yes, probably no. That is a rabbit hole of a question fraught with impenetrable uncertainty. I think the short answer is you were ready to be married in 1964, and I still had law school to go through. After law school, I wasn't really ready to think about marriage until 1971.

<u>Nancy</u>: I was enjoying being single and working, but I was definitely ready. Before meeting Fernando, who was brilliant and charming, I had been in a number of romances. I had thought about marriage more than once to various boys.

<u>Charles</u>: Yes, you told us about Wally Windom.

<u>Nancy</u>: (laughing) But he wasn't the only one I liked.

Charles: Another thing I think is that today we are also different people than we were over fifty years ago. We have more in common now than we had back then. Who knows? That may be part of the secret sauce in 2021. Back in the 1960s, I was a late bloomer, and you were not—and a year older or so to boot. Our internal timeclocks were way out of sync.

Nancy: You could be right. And case in point, I have always been a passionate Democrat, and there is a rumor floating around that you were once a Republican. Chance or timing seems to have been a major player in our lives, if not *the* major player.

Charles: So okay, back to our last stories for this little book, what follows below is the conversation we had some time back about my sleeping custom:

Nancy: (*before turning off the light one night*) Charles, I want you to explain something to me.

Charles: (*yawning*) Okay, what?

Nancy: Well, when you stayed at my house that first night, did you not bring any pajamas with you? You must have owned some.

Charles: I have a feeling you are going somewhere with this. What is your point?

Nancy: Have you always slept in your clothes? When did you start doing that? Did your parents do that? I can't believe they did.

Charles: I'm not really sure, but I always take off my shoes, so I don't get the sheets dirty. You're making it somehow sound like it's weird. And I never, ever wear a hat. You have to admit that.

Nancy: You told me your brother sometimes sleeps in his clothes.

Charles: And in his shoes in that big recliner in front of their TV set. He's not even in bed.

Nancy: It's very odd. It's not completely civilized. People in the civilized world must have been wearing pajamas to bed for a very long time.

Charles: Well, if you are raising an issue of comfort, the T-shirts and sweatpants I wear all day long are completely comfortable at night. I used to change into PJs when I wore jeans with belts or slack pants and shirts that buttoned. At The Reserve, there was no reason to wear anything but sweats and tees.

Nancy: I still don't think it's at all proper or regular.

Charles: Try it sometime. Who knows? You may like it. Might give you a whole new lease on life.

Nancy: (*smiling*) Thanks, but it's not happening.

Charles: Can we close now with your story about your date at the laundromat?

Nancy: Okay, I guess a deal is a deal. I was already out of SMU when this one happened. At SMU, I majored in sociology, and I had a crush on a certain professor (Professor Koenig) in the sociology department who was not especially good-looking, but fascinating, funny, and told great stories. He was also just so smart, and we agreed on the big political issues of the day. Like the Democrat Party.

After I graduated with my degree, I moved into an apartment near the campus. One week I had been procrastinating and procrastinating about doing my laundry, very unlike the present-day Nancy, until it became a dire emergency—all my undies, I mean all, tops and bottoms, were in the laundry bag to be washed! Therefore, I drove to the laundromat with my bag of to-be-washed undies and loaded them into a washer. As I was sitting there, relaxing without underwear reading a magazine, my favorite sociology professor and big crush in my undergraduate days just happened to come strolling by on his way to the famous near-campus beer and pizza hangout, Gordo's, which was next door to the laundromat. He spotted me through the window, came in, grabbed my hand, and pulled me along to have a beer with him and others at Gordo's. I did, sans underwear. What a mix of emotions!

Charles: What happened to your underwear? Did you forget about them in all your excitement? And what did your parents say?

Nancy: No, I picked them up after finishing my beer. They were all completely dry. We had more than one beer. It was a lot of fun. I never told my parents.

Charles: What about the sociology professor? Is there another chapter to this story? Did you ever pick up anyone else at the laundromat after that?

Nancy: Hey, he picked ME up, not the other way around! It was a one-off experience. My ONLY date without undies. He was much older, and I got over the crush.

Finis

Nancy finds unexpected adventure at the laundromat.

APPENDIX

CHARACTERS

Included here are Charles' relatives (a partial list), Nancy's relatives (a partial list), deceased relatives are shown by an asterisk (*), followed by the characters mentioned piece by piece. Note: not all those relatives shown will be mentioned in the stories that follow but are included here because of their importance to Charles and Nancy's lives and stories.

Charles' side: Charles Francis Guittard (author), Mary Lou Kee Guittard*, Clarence Alwin Guittard*, Francis Gevrier (Frank) Guittard*, Josephine Glenn (Mama Josie) Guittard*, John Lester Kee, MD*, Mary Louise (Louise) Roscoe Kee*, John Roscoe Guittard, Jo Harwood Guittard, Mary Louise Guittard Voegtle, Henry J. Voegtle, Jr., Stephen Wood Guittard, Philip Alwin Guittard*, Jim Guittard, Katia Guittard, Katie Guittard, Bob Guittard, Candace Guittard, Miles Guittard, Charlie Guittard, Finn Guittard, Lynn Bussey, Steven Oliver Moffatt, John L. Kee, and Louise Brown Kee.

Nancy's side: Nancy Davis Labastida (author's collaborator), Nancy Virginia Talbot*, Harvey Leo Davis*, Betty X Davis*, Libby Davis*, Virginia Davis Palmer, Harvey Lee Davis, Mark Davis, Charlotte Davis Seifert, Clayton Davis, Talbot Davis, Fernando Labastida*, Fernando Augusto Labastida, Nanette Labastida, Fernando Xavier Labastida, Adriana Labastida, Alejandro Labastida, Eduardo Labastida, Claudia Scalzo, Gabe Scalzo, and Florence Hubbard*.

HOW I GOT POLISHED & WHAT HAPPENED AFTER THAT:

CHARLES' MEMOIR OF GROWING UP

The author: Charles Francis Guittard.

The author's parents: Mary Lou Kee Guittard and Clarence Alwin Guittard.

The author's grandparents: Francis Gevrier Guittard and Josephine Glenn (Mama Josie) Guittard (step-grandmother), and John Lester Kee, MD and Mary Louise Roscoe Kee ("Louise").

The author's siblings: John Roscoe Guittard and Mary Louise Guittard Voegtle.

The author's Guittard cousins: Stephen Wood Guittard and Philip Alwin Guittard.

Wife, writing assistant, and partner of Charles Francis Guittard: Nancy Davis Labastida.

Nancy Davis Labastida's family (parents and siblings mentioned): father Harvey Leo Davis, mother Betty X Davis, sister Virginia Davis Palmer, and brother Harvey Lee Davis.

Acquaintances after law school: Betty, Suzy R–, and Veronica.

Baer, Henry: name partner in McKenzie & Baer and bridge player.

Billy Boastful: According to the author's father, an example of a promising lawyer and politician whose ego got the best of him.

Bridge teachers and authors, international: Charles Goren and Bobby Wolff.

Bridge teachers, local: Mrs. Herbert Wales and Mrs. Nancy Touchstone.

Childhood and high school friends: Arleta Y–, Burt A–, Corky McCord, Dexter B—, Dick Sartain, Eddie Bullman, Jerry G–, Mike Amis, Mike W–, Millie, Robert Knopf, Sid Files, and Tommy Blackshear.

College friends and acquaintances: Larry A–, Bill Hallman.

Composer/author of *Manners Can Be Fun*: Frank Luther.

Dancing partner: Millie.

Dance teachers: Mrs. Finley and Dick Chaplin.

McKenzie, William A.: senior partner of McKenzie & Baer.

McKenzie & Baer: First law firm employing the author.

Parliamentary law teacher of ladies' groups: Mrs. Arthur Harding.

Physicians and other healthcare providers: Nurse Stern, Dr. Strangways, and Dr. Hurt.

Piano teachers: Mrs. Stanley and Mrs. Erna Renard Radke.

Rope trick specialists and childhood heroes: Will Rogers and Will Rogers, Jr.

Social organizations: Dervish Club; Party Service (escorts for social functions).

Speech teachers: Mrs. Bushman (private) and Paul E. Pettigrew (public).

Tennis coaches and retired professionals: Wayne Sabin and Armando Vieira.

Tennis greats: Pancho Gonzales, Ken Rosewall, Margaret Court Smith, and Billie Jean King.

Tennis opponents of note: Harvey Davis (Nancy's brother), Mike Amis, and Steve Lanfer.

"WOW, IT'S ALMOST LIKE WE WALKED HAND IN HAND THROUGH OUR CHILDHOOD!"

A MEMOIR OF A THIRD COURTSHIP & DECEMBER MARRIAGE THAT WASTED NO TIME

Persons mentioned in chronological order in Charles' and Nancy's emails include the following:

Doak Walker, Kyle Rote, Johnny Champion, Dick McKissack, Dr. Aaron Sartain, Richard Sartain, Nancy Swenson, Nancy Penson, Nancy Sommerville, Leo Laborde, Mike Amis, Ham Richardson, Steve Brutsche, Jack Penson, Gordon Galt, Al Oldham, Dr. Hal Moore, Billy Hightower, Mary Guittard Voegtle, Hank Voegtle, Martha Walker, Nancy Richey, Patricia Bernstein, Fernando Labastida, Mary Lou Guittard, Bob Guittard, Frank Guittard, Clarence Guittard, Candace Slaton Guittard, Andre Agassi, Harvey Lee Davis, Betty X Davis, Nancy Reagan, Belva Courts, Roy Rogers, Dale Evans, Ronald Reagan, Clayton Davis, Donald J. Trump, Patricia Verlander Guittard, Steven Moffatt, Mary Hayes, Charlotte Davis Seifert, Robert Benchley, Art Buchwald, Betty White, Claudia Scalzo, Pop and Mama Josie, John Guittard, Steve Guittard, Dr. John Kee, Nipsey Russell, Ralph Edwards, Nancy G–, Nancy B–, Nancy Virginia Talbot, Libby Davis, Mary Louise Davis, Mark Davis, Louise and John Kee, Jo Guittard, Gary Cooper, Nathaniel Branden, Madalyn Murray O'Hair, Wally Amos Criswell, Lara McCrary, John F. Kennedy, Lee Harvey Oswald, Will Rogers, Billy Jordan, Bobby Riggs, Pancho Segura, Armando Vieira, Wayne Sabin, Carl Gregory, Art Wilson, Sue K–, Dick Chaplin, Mrs. Hamilton, Maxyne Cammack, Novak Djokovic, Katie Guittard, John McEnroe, Nanette Labastida, Helen Guittard, Jim Guittard, Katia Guittard, Nicole Holstein, Dr. Aston, Georgette Taylor, Alan Alda, Lynn Bussey, Miles Guittard, Charlie Guittard,

Finn Guittard, Mamie Welhausen Guittard, Jorge and Rosaelena Labastida, Edgar Allan Poe, Darrell–, Broderick Mosley, Telma, Shakespeare, and Uncle Scrooge.

"AND THEN THERE'S THE TIME THAT..."

NANCY'S BEST STORIES: HER MEMOIR OF GROWING UP

Charles Francis Guittard and Nancy Davis Labastida. Other characters in the stories of Nancy Davis Labastida in chronological order: Jim B–, Stella Starr, Ralph Edwards, Betty X Davis, Florence Hubbard, Doak Walker, Jack Benny, Wally Windom, Fernando Augusto Labastida, Fernando Xavier Labastida, Nancy Sinatra, Nancy Davis Reagan, the "little canary," Kenny M–, Weston Wolff, Harvey Lee Davis, Karen S–, Scooter, Candace Montgomery, Allan Gore, Betty Gore, Linda Haire, Roy Rogers, Dale Evans, Trigger, Libby Davis, Lady, Daddy, Virginia Davis Palmer, President McCall, President Neff, Tricky Trixie [not her real name], two Catholic sisters, Xenophon, Nancy's late husband Fernando Labastida, Cuban dictator Batista, Carolyn Calvin, and Talbot Davis.

THE TRIAL OF J. HIRAM HARMLESS

A FANTASY OF A FINAL JUDGMENT DAY

J. Hiram Harmless, the accused and witness in his own behalf.

Jehovah, Panel chair and senior member of the Trinity.

Jesus Christ, Panelist, Jehovah's earthly manifestation; Mary's only son by virgin birth; stepson of Joseph the carpenter.

The Holy Spirit, Panelist, the third person of the Trinity, manifested by the symbols of the wings of a dove and tongues of fire, but otherwise invisible to human beings.

Robert H. Jackson, counsel for the prosecution; formerly lead U.S. prosecutor at the Nuremberg Trials.

Clarence Darrow, counsel for the defense; formerly lead defense counsel in *The State of Tennessee vs. John T. Scopes.*

Mrs. Hortense Heedless, chief witness for the prosecution, ex-wife of the accused, and permanent resident of the Inferno.

INDEX

Names marked shown by an initial (ex., Y–, Arleta) are pseudonyms for the persons' real names.

"Betty" and "Veronica" are pseudonyms when used without last names.

Names followed by "(character)" refer to fictitious characters in the J. Hiram Harmless piece.

Biographies

Charles Francis Guittard

    Charles Francis Guittard is a former attorney-mediator, 2d chair high school trombone player, and bridge and tennis enthusiast. A graduate of Baylor University and Southern Methodist University Law School, he first produced what turned out to be a lifetime writing project, namely, a trilogy focusing on his grandfather and Baylor. The third volume of the trilogy is entitled *I WILL TEACH HISTORY, the Life & Times of Francis Gevrier Guittard, Professor, Baylor University*. The trilogy was inspired by Charles' interest in his grandfather's life along with the twist of fate described in the third volume which changed everything. The current work of stories is the result of Charles' collaboration with wife Nancy Davis Labastida, whom he persuaded to add her own stories of growing up to his own lest they all should be forever lost to the past's dark vault. Charles has three adult children and four grandchildren.

Nancy Davis Labastida

Nancy Labastida is one of eight children born in Chicago to law professor and tennis player Harvey Leo Davis and Betty X Davis, a thrifty woman of many talents, writing being one of them. Nancy is a sociology graduate of Southern Methodist University in Dallas, a civil rights activist during her college days, a Democrat, and an avid reader. Before she married Charles Francis Guittard, she was married for 54 years to Fernando Labastida, an attorney for the United Nations. She spent many years living in Manhattan, New York, and London, England, before retiring to Austin, Texas. Nancy grew up competing at swimming, bridge, tennis (she achieved fame both as a junior and then senior tennis player), *Password*, *Scrabble*, and *Wheel of Fortune*. Nancy is a born raconteur with an unusual memory. Nancy has two children and six adult grandchildren, including one grandson with special needs. Shortly after they married in 2021, Charles started making notes on her stories of growing up in Dallas.

Amanda Hope Colborn

Illustrator

Amanda Hope Colborn lives with her husband, Chad, in Bryan, Texas. She is currently pursuing her Master of Arts in illustration from Savannah College of Art and Design. Amanda graduated from Baylor University in 2022 with a BFA in Studio Art. Her work was selected for the Baylor Juried Student Art Exhibition in 2020, 2021, 2022, and won best in printmaking for 2022. Amanda enjoys hiking, playing board games, and spending time with friends and family.

Made in the USA
Las Vegas, NV
05 March 2024

86244879R00174